RECIPE FOR EMPATHY

DEBORAH BAKTI

To David & Donna,
Thank you for being
an inspiration and
guides !

Deborah

To Ty, Taylor and Logan

"I think we all have empathy. We may not have enough courage to display it."

— MAYA ANGELOU

"You can only understand people if you feel them in yourself."

— JOHN STEINBECK

**In a world that's transactional, be different.
Be relational.**

We live in a fast-paced world now. I'm not telling you anything you don't realize yourself. We find it challenging to slow down, pay attention and be interested in one another. Instead of composing our responses carefully, we often react without pause to consider how our actions might be interpreted or how they might affect someone. Feeling misperceived or misunderstood, or worse, like someone doesn't care about understanding you, can crack the foundation of trust that every relationship, those with acquaintances and intimates, are built upon. Our failure to see one another, to make the quality of engagement we have with others our highest priority, shows up in the weakening of really important interactions: in our homes with our children, in our communities with neighbours and friends, and in our places of work.

Without careful attention to how our responses land and without the intention to project empathy we don't put ourselves in the other person's shoes, and we fail to connect. That loss of connection caused by the absence of empathy is what we are blaming smart phones, technology and any other modern inventions for.

But we have the ability to do things differently.

We can seek out opportunities to be relational with one another, by bringing awareness of other people's perceptions or experiences of us back to the forefront of our minds. It isn't just you, it's all of us. In the places where we congregate, at dinner tables, restaurants, and in community spaces, our lost skills are showing, and these are where the greatest opportunities reside. The **RECIPE for Empathy** is about adjusting some of the ways that you relate to others. It is about being more aware of and attentive to your reactions and how others might be experiencing you. It's about being more intentional with how you show up and how you are being with people. It's about paying attention to and being interested in making connections and being relational with people, especially when it matters the most.

The RECIPE offers strategies for bringing empathy into your seniors' care workplace where residents, families and staff will all benefit. There is a crisis in seniors' care and I'm not talking about the one you think. We sometimes forget why we got into this work in the first place, when we are caught up in the transactional nature of health care. The focus on connection and empathy has been one of the costs of change. And it's no wonder, because the demands in the sector are greater than ever, by nearly any measure.

Management, staff and even families of residents know the current pressures of long-term care operations. The acuity level of residents is increasing, putting pressure on the staffing levels, and recruiting for health human resources in seniors' care is an ongoing challenge because they are challenging jobs. As our population continues to age, there is an increased demand to redevelop older homes and build new ones. The need for seniors' care isn't going away. There are 263,000 long-term care beds in Canada, and some 77,000 of those are in Ontario, the province in which I live, where

- 85% of residents need extensive help with daily activities such as getting out of bed, eating, or toileting; 1 in 3 are highly or entirely dependent on staff,
- 90% of residents have some form of cognitive impairment; 1 in 3 are severely impaired,
- 46% of residents exhibit some level of aggressive behaviour related to their cognitive impairment or mental health condition,
- 40% of residents have a mood disorder such as anxiety, depression, bipolar disorder, or schizophrenia, and
- 40% of residents need monitoring for an acute medical condition.[1]

We have this perfect storm of increasing need for seniors' care, decreasing availability of health care staff and rising costs that put pressure on funding resources.

Long-term care is a 24/7, 365-days-a-year operation, that deals with death on a regular basis. It's not uncommon for a home to experience half of its residents passing away during the year. The types of clinical supports being provided in long-term care and even retirement homes today were typically done in hospitals just a short few years ago. The acuity and complexity of care needs are demanding a higher level of skills and knowledge from the staff in homes, while residents and families still expect a personable approach. The pace of work, with the litany of tasks and documentation required by regulatory bodies, is unrelenting. The day-to-day tasks are still required while residents, families and staff grieve the ongoing losses that occur, and must readjust to new residents and families coming into their community.

Families come into the home environment with a mixture of trepidation and relief. They would rather not need your services at all. They may be in denial of the reality of their circumstances, burdened by a myriad of emotions that bring a different level of pressure and tension to your home, as they try to find their way in this new role of being a resident's wife, husband, partner, son, daughter.

What can happen is that your home – where you work, where residents live and where families visit, can become a setting for drama and conflict, as these 'by need and necessity' relationships begin and end.

These are environments of constant change. Residents pass away, and their families no longer come to the home, (unless they continue to volunteer). Staff leave, new staff start, and with those changes, residents and families try to cope with getting to know who's providing the care now, and how that will feel. As residents' conditions worsen, the staff need to manage the increased care needs, and the families are torn apart watching their loved one decline, fearing and anticipating that final day.

No wonder we are seeing increasing levels of burnout and frustration with staff. You are just trying to keep up with the increasing demands and pressures of the system. At the same time, you have the emotions of residents and families to work with, as they struggle with all this personal change happening in their lives.

And yet, the work you do matters. Providing care and

compassion to aging and ailing seniors, as well as to their families during this challenging time in their lives, matters. And being there for each other, as people who are providing this much needed care, matters.

And that's what this book is about – how to be relational, to connect with care and compassion, with each other as humans, making a difference, and making moments that matter.

CONTENTS

WHERE WE STARTED

When my husband Ty went into long-term care, we had no idea how long he would live there. Ty had convinced himself that he would get better and come home, even though doctors had told us the disease was degenerative, incurable, and fatal. I'm not sure what I believed.

This home was our first choice, of the few we had on our list. But any home for your loved one is a forced choice; one we never *want* to make. I knew this was a move that needed to be made, but I could never have envisioned this as our future.

We had been white knuckling through the intensive care needs at home, when the phone call came that a bed was available for him in this home. Ty's needs and addressing them to best of our ability, never mind the emotional 'death by a thousand cuts' journey had become our new normal over three years. That call felt like a lifeline that came with sadness and grief, yet some sense of relief washed over me. I'd been so worried about the next phase of his health care, and I felt such uncertainty about what we might need to do to keep him safe and comfortable as his condition declined, while we continually tried our best to adapt to the next stage of increasing demands these changes brought.

When he was receiving home care, we were still all together in our home. Yes, it was disruptive having someone arrive every day to help Ty with his morning routine, while our kids were getting ready to go to school and I was trying to get out the door for my long commute. But we drew comfort from these routines and the familiarity of being in our home together, while being acutely aware that this was not sustainable.

Moving to long-term care meant this home routine was ending for all of us. It meant that things were progressing in a direction we would rather have denied. Ty was moving into a care facility, an institution with 143 other residents who also needed a higher level of care than their families and care supports could provide.

No one ever looks forward to this time, this move or this reality. No one typically thinks *"Boy, when I grow old, or get sick and can't take care of myself, I can't wait to move into a seniors' care home"*, after all.

Moving into seniors' care is like entering into a relationship with people you'd rather not have to meet and work with, but you must. The home's staff are providing a service that your family needs for your loved one's safety, comfort and quality of life, but they are strangers in the midst of your most intimate, treasured relationships. You've gotten to the point where you can't do it alone, and it's putting you and your family, as well as your loved one in a tenuous and unsustainable position. This is difficult to navigate for everyone, the resident, family and the staff at the home, and that first day, the admission day bears the greatest strain of all.

Even though the average length of stay continues to shorten due to more frailty and health complexities, homes can have residents living there from weeks to years, even decades. This place is the residents' home now, where the families come to visit their loved ones. What a challenge these complex emotions present. Seniors' care providers are also challenged to merge a bustling workplace with the feel of a home, toward the goal that families feel welcome in the space their loved one now lives and receives essential health care.

I tended to think of the home as a little town with many roles, activities and dynamics at play. It's a work environment for the staff, where they are scheduled, expected to perform their job duties while being compassionate and caring with their vulnerable residents, who are in need of regular support.

The residents are dealing with their own challenges, and in most cases, they'd rather be at home if they could, but their health deficits have brought them here. Families come and go, bringing their myriad of emotions and expectations with them, which in themselves can create conflict but also, on a good day, some pleasant exchanges and experiences.

There are other 'forces' at play. Let's not forget the rules and requirements that are mandated and monitored through regulatory bodies. You also have your corporate office that sends through directives or new procedures to follow, one more thing that must get done during an already busy day. Some days have multiple major tasks in addition to daily operations and then a surprise gets added to it. You have a new admission, training to be rolled out, or maybe, a Ministry or other regulatory inspector shows up.

I couldn't predict how long Ty would be living in the home, or how long I'd live in this new role as a resident's wife. But I did have the awareness that this could likely be a longer term arrangement and the sense that I'd need to figure things out and fit in. I was going to need relationships with staff who would be an extension of the best possible care I could ensure for my husband. I wanted my relationships in the home to be positive, healthy and supportive ones. I just had no idea how that was going to work or how it would integrate into our already strained lives.

I'd been aware of the transactional nature of our interactions in hospitals and with clinical specialists since Ty first became ill, but going into those experiences, I knew that my interface with those staff and medical personnel would be limited in length, possibly only lasting the duration of an appointment. The end game in that stage of Ty's health care journey was diagnosis and purpose-driven interactions were the norm. It was always nice to have encouraging conversations and feel good moments, of course, but generally speaking, they were a means toward the end of getting a diagnosis so we could 'move on' with our lives.

With Ty moving into long-term care, that meant we were moving him and the belongings he could take with him, to live in that building, share a semi-private room with another man, and entrusting the staff with his safety, care and quality of life. And even though I worked in the sector and understood seniors' care from a business perspective, I was going in blind (for the first and hopefully only time) as a resident's wife.

At the time Ty was admitted, my dad was already living in a long-term care facility on the other side of the city. He'd been admitted three months previously, and although I assisted with the paperwork and application process, my mom took the lead. I'd had my hands full with managing Ty's care then. Regretfully, I look back wishing I had spent more time visiting my dad there and was probably perceived as the 'absent daughter'.

Most families are going in blind, not really knowing how to play the 'family member' role, what to anticipate or what is expected of them. I believe it's imperative to help them step into this new role more effectively, with empathy and education so that there is a better opportunity to have healthy relationships and connection from the very start. After all, when we start a new job, there is an onboarding process – an orientation and 'here's how things work around here'. Becoming a family member is taking on a new role, and without having the playbook, it doesn't always go so smoothly.

Ty lived in long-term care for four years, before passing away in April 2015. He was 63-years old when he became a resident, younger in comparison to the typical resident's age. He was a strong-willed, determined, fun-loving troublemaker who gave the staff a run for their money on most days. He loved to wheel out those front doors and either head over to the variety store to buy cigarettes or propel himself to the local pub for a few beers with the regulars. He was an 'exit seeking eloper' in care parlance, who would always answer his cell phone when the staff called him to find out where he was this time.

He also liked to monopolize the TV in the library and either watch mob movies (at the loudest possible volume, because he was deaf in one ear) or play video games that were quite frankly, inappropriate to some of the female residents who happened to wander in to see what was going on. Ty was an extrovert, so all the residents and most families, and of course, all the staff and management knew him.

When he heard there was a resident who passed, he would call me in tears to tell me about it and how much he was going to miss that individual, and then he'd head down to the front foyer and wait for the family to arrive. He wanted to give his condolences and make sure the family knew how wonderful their loved one was. This was Ty's home and his community. He was a larger than life personality who drove everyone crazy (including me and the kids) while winning them over with his charm, humour and big heart.

Imagine the number of interactions, transactions, experiences, conversations, frustrations, tears, minor conflicts, problems to solve and successful resolutions that happened in those four years. Yet these were my husband's final years, and this was where the kids and I spent time with him. There were so many moments that mattered – moments that transcended the necessary and went beyond the transactional nature that seniors' care can sometimes feel like. Those are the moments that create the positive ripples when stories are shared, and acknowledgements are made. They are like deposits in the relational bank account that can counterbalance some of the times when things don't go so well.

After Ty passed away, and the kids and I focused on pivoting yet again, this time as a family of three, I continued to work at my job at Extendicare. As the Vice President of Human Resources, I would be brought into performance issues within the homes that sometimes led to discipline or termination. And these would typically involve the grievance and even the arbitration process to resolve. Quite often, these issues stemmed from family members voicing their concerns and looking for resolution. I'd seen this from both sides of the relationship now. There was no going back for me.

I could relate to how the families felt, and I was frustrated that there wasn't a better way for the families and staff to be able to relate to each other and work in collaboration and partnership. The irony of working in an industry where I became a customer didn't escape me.

I had the vantage point that most people don't— instant access to work colleagues that knew the ins and outs of home care, long-term care and retirement. And even with that advantage, I still faced struggles to navigate, communicate and manage these significant life and health transitions. I will forever be grateful for the guidance and support my work colleagues gave me during this time and the care and compassion that was given to Ty while he lived in long-term care. When I look big picture of the four years he resided in that home, overall there were more positives than negatives.

There were missed opportunities to be relational, to connect as human beings, and these are the times that can send people sideways, resulting in them reacting strongly, perhaps disproportionately, to the situation. That's where the opportunity to transform families into fans lays—in those moments that matter—with intention and purpose.

THE ROAD TO THE RECIPE

**I saw the opportunity for the conversation
to expand, and the RECIPE for Empathy
was born, from the need for practical
approaches, tools and insights.**

I have been a participant in both sides of the seniors' care
industry for the last thirteen years—the corporate side and the
client side.

I knew the experience with my dad who had Parkinson's and
Lewy Body, whose needs moved him from home care to acute care,
and into long-term care where he lived for six months before he
passed away. I helped my mom transition to retirement then assisted
living and now in memory care.

My husband Ty was diagnosed with a rare illness that caused
such a significant and rapid decline in his health that he required
full time care when he was only 63-years-old, and he became a
long-term care home resident. During those years, I worked as a
corporate executive with Extendicare, a major provider in the

same health care industry that was having a huge impact on my family's life. This knowledge of both sides of the seniors' care world made me something of a 'go-to person' for friends and extended family dealing with aging or ailing family members and struggling to make the difficult yet necessary decisions around their care. My work 'in the system' qualified me somehow, and my experience with my dad amplified my 'know-how', but nothing prepared me for the day my husband's needs plunged us into the admissions process of long-term care. That part of my experience has brought me to the work I do now and to writing **RECIPE for Empathy**.

When I left my corporate job in 2017, my kids were grown and moved out, and my husband had died two years earlier. Departing the corporate world to become a consultant was not a decision I made lightly. I was called to new work. I had learned and seen so much as a family member. I felt strongly that if I combined my knowledge from both sides of seniors' care, I could improve the experience for others. I wanted to take all of the stories that I had gathered through the chaos of being a resident's wife, as well as other family's experiences, and share them as insights to create a better workplace for staff and improve experiences for residents and their families within the seniors' care environment.

Steve Jobs said, "You can't connect the dots looking forward; you can only connect them looking backwards. So, you have to trust that the dots will somehow connect in your future. You have to trust in something – your gut, destiny, life, karma, whatever."[1]

The dots that led to the writing of this book appeared during a dinner conversation with a colleague. It was a few months after Ty had passed away, and as our conversation meandered through how I was 'dealing' with his passing, she asked about our admission day experience. I reflected on that most difficult, heartbreaking day, and described for her how it felt like a transaction we were being processed through. I recalled the sights and smells, the busyness and the distraction, and our feeling that we were on a production line-- get the new resident admitted, complete the piles of paperwork, check the boxes.

With tears in her eyes, she said, "I feel so ashamed because we do that to families every... single... day."

My memories, drawn out of me in a conversation by a kind, truly interested colleague sparked the message of this book and ultimately, the passion I feel about bringing a focus on empathy back to seniors' care.

Of course, I didn't know it at the time, but this was one of Steve Jobs' dots on the path that contributed to my decision to leave my corporate job and dedicate my work to helping seniors' care providers create stronger, healthier, more vibrant and positive relationships with their families.

Admissions day focus

I CHOSE the admissions day as an illustration for the elements of the RECIPE because that day, and the days and weeks after, when the family is simply trying to adapt and adjust to this new way of life, are critical predictors of whether this relationship flourishes or flounders. The experience the family has with the staff in the home in the early days is the stage setter, because those moments of first impressions can be so instrumental in forecasting how the interactions between staff, residents and their families will be received and either reacted or responded to in future. I felt confident of this when I reflected on my own experience on my husband's move-in day. Had those initial days and weeks when I was trying to find my way in my new identity as a resident's wife gone differently, an even more positive and engaging experience during the four years that my husband lived in long-term care might have resulted.

Although one of dozens a home might do in a year, that admissions day was life altering for us on our arduous journey with diagnosis and treatment up until that point. When the team arrived and they were rushed and distracted I found it difficult to wear only my corporate hat and give them the benefit of my knowledge that they work in an incredibly challenging environment, because I was a wife then, on one of the most difficult days of our lives.

Of course, I got it. They had full work days and heads full of problems more challenging than this admission. And I certainly felt it. I saw how some of them looked over our heads through the glass window behind us, where residents were grouped in a circle watching TV. I felt like we were just another transaction that they needed to 'get done' that day, and that they wanted to get through all of the required paperwork and procedures as quickly as they could. I felt like they had done this a thousand times before, and we were just one more family, one more checklist of disquieting questions that they were unable to soften the impact of for us, either by waiting or asking more sensitively. Do not resuscitate orders, and rapid-fire yeses and noes about his personal care needs kept coming.

I knew this had to get done. After all I was a person who worked in the same government-regulated industry, but I was also in the role of the wife of a very ill man who was being admitted.

Because the admission day is the most challenging to handle well, with the dual burdens of process and propriety, both families and staff bringing with them their own list of needs, my conviction arose--if the first day goes well, and home staff lay a solid foundation of care and connection, so much more about the experience will be improved for both staff and families.

You see, on my husband's admission day, staff in the long-term care home couldn't know what it felt like from our side. They couldn't have known the number of conversations we'd had with medical people who made us feel 'handled', 'informed', and 'processed' this way before. They couldn't have known the mixture of emotions that my husband and I carried with us into that room.

Or, could they?

I concluded later, that with some effort, and with some awareness, they certainly could have. If they had treated us differently then, establishing an openness to connection, I reasoned innumerable times over the following months, their attentiveness to our fear, pain and angst could have lessened the tension for all of us, and perhaps turned this moment of dread into one that was at least more comfortable, if not somewhat comforting or even hopeful, for us. And the foundation of trust, respect and partnership between us could have been laid, easing the bumps and challenges that inevitably arise within seniors' care.

What you can expect from *RECIPE for Empathy*

I CREATED THE RECIPE FRAMEWORK, then this book, with the seniors' care environment in mind, based on my personal and professional experiences. Here are some of the benefits that I believe readers will take away from the book:

- Know how to build strong foundations for healthy family relationships
- Discover ways to create trust and avoid friction, conflict and escalations
- Be able to create and contribute to a more pleasant work environment
- Learn ways to build your bandwidth so that you can be less reactive when under stress and respond more effectively
- Understand how slowing down can actually create more efficiency and effectiveness
- Be aware of how connecting and relating to others improves your sense of well-being and happiness (When you do good, you feel good)
- Get practical and easy-to-implement ideas that you can start applying right away
- Learn how to step out of auto pilot or reactive mode and be more mindful and intentional with how you interact with others
- Gain ideas on how to reduce the drama in your

workplace so that you have more energy for your
residents and families, and yourself

- Recognize complaints as commitments, and be equipped
to respond more effectively to create resolution faster

MORE THAN ANYTHING, I hope that this book will inspire change in
your life, not just your workplace. Some of the significant outcomes
that are possible from these pages are shifts in your

- perspective with the family's journey, and your mindset,
beliefs and behaviours,
- understanding, ability and desire to relate to others – to
be relational, and
- experience of more joy and satisfaction with your
relationships as you practice these principles.

FIRST IMPRESSIONS

A t some point on the drive to the long-term care home on admission day, the impact of what was happening hit me— my husband was going to be living there, staying there, and not coming home to live with me and the kids again. He was going to be taken care of by other people and no longer by us or the home care PSW's. He would be living in a room with a man he'd never met before, where he couldn't even lock the door. Everything that would happen in Ty's life from that day forward, was going to happen there. He would decline there, to the point that he would need other people to help wash, dress and feed him. How do you even wrap your head around that?

I wasn't able to dig down for the small upsides on that day. Later I would find them, and console myself that the change had been for his safety and health. But on that day, I badgered myself with questions for the hundredth time about whether I was doing the right, best thing or not. I felt so sad, guilt-ridden and helpless about the choice. I wasn't yet able to recognize the toll it had been taking on me to work full-time and keep up with the kids' needs while functioning sleep deprived and emotionally defeated. I was concerned about how to stay strong for them, how to keep managing as a single-parent in Ty's absence and take on this new resident's wife role. On that drive and on the walk behind his wheelchair into the home, I could only run through how terrible this felt – and wonder how he felt about becoming a resident in a nursing home and how this disruption in our family's life was going to affect us. The reality that my husband was about to become a resident had me feeling unhinged. I was going to have to leave him there that day, in his new home. This was also the place where he was going to die.

I share this personal backstory to provide you with a glimpse of the mental state I was in as I wheeled my husband up to the reception desk on move-in day. I could also add that we had been through a few years of Ty's steady health decline, including a lengthy and convoluted path to his diagnosis with a rare disease, hundreds of medical appointments, nearly thirty specialists and six major hospitals. What is important to gather here is that every family's story is as unique as they are, and the choice to admit each resident has likely been preceded by an indirect and complicated path. Some new residents will have come directly from their family homes, while others may have come from hospital, a retirement home or another long-term care facility. Together with their families, they will each be carrying the weight of their journey, and the collective experiences that have defined their passage.

The irony wasn't lost on me, as we sat in the family meeting room waiting for a meeting we didn't want but needed to have. I'd visited many long-term care and retirement homes in my corporate capacity, and there I was – not in the role of a corporate employee, but now as a family member, on what was for me one of the most difficult, heartbreaking days of my life, looking at long-term care from the other side. There was no way I would ever regain professional distance from the complicated emotional landscape.

I tried some pathetic small talk (no easy feat for an introvert), engaging Ty on the weather, sports, and how maybe he could play the piano that was sitting in the room. Small talk with the man I had been married to at that time for twenty-five years - the anxiety was overwhelming. I looked out and watched staff and residents walking and wheeling by, taking in the sounds, smells and activities of what clearly was a busy, bustling place.

When the Director of Care (DOC) and a few others arrived, I barely took in what they said by way of introduction. I had met the DOC before, and I'm sure they told us their names. I do know that one of them apologized for being late and said, "you know, there's always something going on around here," because my defensive thought immediately was, Really? You know what? There's a lot going on with us too!

It began with the DOC flipping open a file and with pen poised over a stack of papers, she led the process. "Let's review what medications you are taking" and "Do you prefer a bath or a shower?"

Then there were the questions about toileting and personal care, financials, emergency contacts - questions that felt awkward with Ty sitting right there, trying to process everything. I wondered if it was too much to expect that they'd have some sense of our discomfort, even if they did not have any knowledge of our life circumstances. I wondered if I was expecting too much.

And then the really awkward question, posed to me: "If something happens, do you want us to resuscitate him?"

I knew these were questions required by the Ministry, but I couldn't believe they were being asked just minutes after arrival. I reminded myself, more than once, that they were doing their job. But what I was feeling in this meeting overpowered all rational thought. I was the wife of a 63-year-old man being admitted to a facility because of his rapidly deteriorating mobility and brain health. I could feel a meltdown rising but focused on holding it together in front of Ty and these strangers. But I was not okay. My breakdown happened later when I got home to the space no longer occupied by my husband.

This was my first impression – and how I felt is something that I remember clearly even now eight years later. What I felt from their energy and body language was that we were just another transaction like they had done innumerable times before. We were just another meeting that needed to get done that day. It was painfully familiar.

We had been through so many meetings in our health care system where the detached, required routine and data gathering, and form filling were the prime objectives for medical professionals.

You've Got Seven Seconds

THERE's some debate over how long it takes for a person to size up whether they like or trust someone or not. Some articles say we have seven seconds to influence the impact we have on people. According to others, it takes just a tenth of a second to form an impression of someone you've just met. The old adage is still as true as it ever was--first impressions are super important, and it's well worth your time and attention to be intentional with how you create one.

Humans are hardwired to quickly assess new situations and react with an "I do or I don't feel safe with you", or an "I do or I don't trust you."

You can be intentional with the kind of first impression you want to make. You can influence the mood of the meeting and avoid any snap judgments and impressions that could send the relationship sideways.

When the stress response is triggered, you feel it in your body. You notice your heart rate increasing, or you feel your temperature rise. Perhaps your face gets flushed, or you feel a cold flash course through your body. Your fight or flight response has been prompted and your natural inclination will be to either emotionally detaching yourself or physically leaving. The fight or flight response is a protection mechanism. It's our warning signal to deal with what we perceive as impending danger.

Think about it this way. If the family had it their way, they wouldn't need the services of a long-term care home for their loved one. Mom or Dad would be able to remain at home. But aging and ailing health has forced this decision to be made. And they are likely feeling resistance to this forced change, wishing they could wave a magic wand and make this reality go away.

Think of a time when you had a medical appointment or needed to get test results, and you didn't want to go but knew you needed to? Or when you've needed surgery and although you understood it was necessary you would certainly have preferred not to endure the discomfort and recovery. Put yourself in the families' shoes; try to imagine what they are feeling as they manage their own emotions on admission day, starting down a whole new path, without the option to circle back to their former version of normal. Their new normal wasn't something they ever anticipated for their mother, father, husband, wife, sister, brother, aunt, or uncle before he or she got sick or declined into a state where their health needed 'institutional care'.

There is no playbook for this new normal.

They have been thrown into this situation and have to figure out how it works, while grappling with the myriad of conflicting emotions and the emotional and logistical turmoil that brings.

You know your home inside and out – it's where you work, a place you're familiar and comfortable with. And you know all of the wonderful (as well as the not so wonderful) people and activities that happen there. For your new family this is a whole new world that has likely been forced upon them because of illness and need. Their lives have been disrupted and they likely feel displaced, discombobulated and disappointed.

Responding, Reacting and Residue

"I've learned that people will forget what you said, people will forget what you did, but people will never forget how you made them feel." [1] – Maya Angelou

IT's no secret--you're busier than ever. And seniors' care is an exceptionally busy environment. Those of you who work in seniors' care don't have much time between tasks. You go in to work every day knowing that you'll be faced with competing priorities, and you consistently scramble to stay one step ahead of a potential mess.

Too many tasks, not enough time. Am I right?

You have a million things on your mind, task lists a mile long, and you're moving through your day, interacting or transacting with all sorts of people – staff, residents, vendors, and families. There are so many situations that can pull your attention away from the tasks at hand. Even if you begin your day with the best of intentions and a great sense of urgency, sometimes the requirements of reacting to multiple demands, and the frenzy of fire-fighting, tilt your best laid plans sideways.

Maybe you had an unpleasant conversation with a family member who was disappointed to find that her mom's hair wasn't done or her teeth brushed, when she showed up for a visit. This encounter might have left you with many feelings that are reflected in your presence even though you'd prefer they not show. The effort to suppress what you're feeling impacts your energy level and ability to focus.

What you're feeling is going to show up somehow, despite your best efforts.

What can happen, is that you bring that negative, stress-laden energy with you to the next meeting or interaction. The residue of the last interaction, comes with you, making you seem preoccupied or disinterested in the people you've just joined.

I recall one day when I was working in my seniors' care corporate role, swimming in the constant flow of meetings, conference calls, and conversations, where my greatest hope was that an early end or late start to a meeting might allow for a bathroom break, and every single minute was booked. I had started with my predictable running stance and relied on caffeine and urgency--the dopamine hit we get from solving problems and adrenaline, to get me through.

I remember noticing how the first conversation of my day set the tone for the rest of it. That was the day that some brave soul dared to ask me if I'd gotten up on the wrong side of the bed. I saw how I was absorbing the energy, mindset and mood that was being created from that first interaction in my workday, and I was lugging it around with me like a lead weight to my other meetings and conversations. As I left my first meeting and went into the next, I was aware of the residue of emotion, and how it was impacting my mood and my ability to fully be present and participatory the rest of the day.

Do you ever catch yourself sitting in a meeting, in your shift huddle, or talking to a co-worker or resident, and you're thinking about a phone call you need to make, a task your boss assigned you in the last meeting, or you're mentally going over a disagreement that happened before you even got to work? It can be really difficult to maintain focus when you're stewing about a challenging issue that needs your attention. This state that you're in can become a source of distraction and frustration for both you and those you are with now, because even though you're physically present, you're not mentally there – you're checked out and they are expecting you to be attentive.

Let's turn the meeting room table around for a moment. Haven't you seen this yourself? Perhaps you've been in a meeting, or at a gathering of people, when a person joins and you either feel the positive vibes vacate the room, or the energy of the room elevates with their entrance.

In an admissions day scenario, consider how this might play out from the perspective of the family of a new resident. These are your customers coming into your long-term care home, unaware of what kind of day you or the other team members are having. It's safe to assume that they woke up not particularly excited about how this day would unfold. They probably feel quite unprepared to navigate through this day with all of their conflicting emotions and lack of knowledge about how the system works. They are quite likely hoping for some reassurance that they've made the right decision for their loved one by coming to your home.

I can tell you, even now, eight years later, the day I sat in our admissions meeting at the home where my husband was going to be living, I felt so stressed and tightly wound myself, and I got the clear impression from the staff in attendance that they had other things to do, and many other, possibly more important things on their minds. It seemed like our admission meeting was an interruption to their day, one that was going to eat up a lot of time and they were thinking about that.

For staff members, this is one of many interactions – or 'transactions' they need to complete. For the family, this could be the first time, maybe the only time that they will be admitting a family member to a long-term care home – it's a highly emotional experience for them. How staff members show up (mood, demeanour, level of distraction or attention), can be felt and observed, and it can change the outcome for everyone. And it can create this residue that sticks. Has this ever been your experience with an admissions meeting? Is this a situation you've been in? Maybe you've walked into an admissions meeting after sorting out a resident issue or receiving a family complaint, some grievance or dispute or an unpleasant email or phone call. Or you are introduced to your new resident and family as they are quickly being navigated through the admissions day process. You haven't taken the opportunity to rid yourself of the residue from that earlier situation and you are not bringing fresh energy with you as you meet this new family, and they will feel it.

Research shows that the more emotional the impact of a memory, whether positive or negative, the more vividly we recall its details and the more likely it will be stored in long-term memory. This is why we remember where we were and what we were doing when significant events happen – think of world events like when Kennedy was shot, or 9-11, or where you were when you heard about the tsunami in Thailand or Prince's death. What about family events like the moment you got the call that your mom had a stroke? Take a moment now and think about a significant event that happened, or one you heard about, and what you were doing and how it felt. I distinctly remember what I was doing when I saw the news of Lady Diana's fatal car accident in Paris in 1997. I was 8 ¾ months pregnant and couldn't sleep due to my hugeness and discomfort. So, there I was in the early morning hours watching TV and the breaking news came across the screen. To this day when I see news articles or TV clips of Lady Diana I go back to that moment of feeling complete disbelief and sadness for the loss of this amazing person.

Emotional memories are encoded deeply within us.

Assume that the family you're meeting will remember the feelings of this day forever and remember how they felt based on the environment that you can help create for them.

When I meet with families and I ask them to share their first day story, to talk about how they brought their loved one in to live as a resident, and to tell me how it felt, I usually hear things like,

"It was so hard, and overwhelming."

"The day was so exhausting."

"I felt nervous, emotional and overwhelmed."

"I felt like a failure. I should have been able to keep caring for them"

They don't recall the paperwork, rules and requirements, or names of everyone they meet. What they remember is how they felt, how they were treated, and how supported and acknowledged they felt.

Families feel a wide variety of emotions that can range from guilt to relief. Families can also feel grateful and appreciative that their loved one, who may have spent a great deal of time on a wait list, or crisis list, finally got 'selected', and will now get the level of care required. The families may feel like the burden of caregiving is now being lifted but there may also be fear around giving up control of providing the care, particularly if they have been on the front lines with their loved one.

We can't know what people are feeling when they come into the admissions meeting, but we can assume they will benefit from our empathy.

Think about the last time you had an unpleasant interaction with a family member. Perhaps it was how you felt they spoke to you, or their body language that made you feel uncomfortable. Now consider the interaction again--what are you actually reflecting on in looking at that memory? It's likely you're thinking about how it felt when they raised their voice or remembering vividly the look of frustration on their face, the way they pointed their finger at you, challenging you about something you just said. On the flip side, think about the last time someone complimented you. Maybe one of your resident's daughters told you how great you are with her mom, and how "Mom's face lights up when you walk into the room". Are you focusing on the words, or how you felt when they shared these sentiments about you?

We are human beings, not human doings And a big part of our humanity is remembering how we feel when we are connecting with others.

A concept, based on a quote that is often attributed to Victor E Frankl, author of *Man's Search for Meaning*, suggests that there is a space between stimulus and response where a choice exists. The choice we make, how we choose to respond is the ultimate predictor of the nature of the outcome, which may be growth and freedom. Each of us has a choice, in every interaction—to react or to respond. It is all about the space. {...}

What I believe Frankl was saying, is that each of us has a choice, in every interaction—we can choose to either react or respond.

A reaction is something that occurs when we are not mindful and allow the situation to take control. It's when we are just falling into the path of what's happening. Without thought.

Without a plan. Without awareness.

A response is thoughtful and deliberate. A response involves a conscious choice, it reflects mindful consideration, and your intention to be empathetic has an opportunity to reveal itself.

Another book that showed up at the right time for me was *The Power of TED* The Empowerment Dynamic* by David Emerald. I was feeling pretty beaten up with the stress and strain of our situation when I learned about the Drama Triangle and the Empowerment Dynamic, and how we can take steps to recognize which space we are living in, and to consciously choose to step out of the victim mindset and into the creator mindset.

When we are in a victim mindset, one of the roles we can play in the Dreaded Drama Triangle, we focus on the problems, whereas when we are in a creator mindset, our focus is on the outcome.

Choosing to shift your focus from problems to outcomes also shifts how you feel and how you relate and connect with those around you, as well as giving you a choice to respond versus react to whatever you're dealing with. This book helped me to see more clearly what I could impact and influence and how it all started with me choosing what I was going to focus on, how I was going to relate to my circumstances and people around me, and what actions I was going to take. I didn't always get it right of course, but I was so impacted by this book, that I became a certified practitioner and trained hundreds of leaders and team members where I worked.

We always have choice in how we show up and connect with others, and the memories we create based on how we are either being relational or transactional. Either way, you are leaving an impression so why not be intentional with it?

**People will remember the way
you make them feel.**

RESET

SHAKE OFF THE RESIDUE

"You can't calm the storm so stop trying. What you can do is calm yourself. The storm will pass."

— TIMBER HAWKEYE

When we pay attention to other people's feelings as well as tapping into how we feel at the moment, we are on the pathway of choosing to *reset*. Resetting is a process of shaking off the residue of what went before, paring away the distractedness that can give other people the impression that we are disinterested.

I've created a reset tool that I call PORCH. It's a great way to take the path of responding versus reacting. (You can even imagine yourself sitting on a porch, in a comfortable arm chair, looking at the situation at hand, and take these steps.)

Let's use the example of an upset family member who has just approached you to talk about a concern they have. A resident's daughter has just arrived to visit her mom. She goes into the room and within seconds it seems, she comes out with an angry look on her face. You see her looking around, she spots you, and she walks right up to you and with a tone of frustration says,

"When was my mom's brief changed last? I just checked it and it's wet".

P: Pause

This can take just a second or two – to take a breath – as you may have just tightened up to brace yourself. This pause can let your nervous system know everything is okay. Breathe.

O: Observe

As you're breathing, keep yourself in the observer mindset – your role right now is to notice what's being said, how it's being said, and not get entangled or absorbed into the other person's emotion and state of mind. The only way you can be of service, remain emotionally detached and not get sucked into going reactive is to put yourself in the audience and observe what's unfolding.

R: Reflect

Maybe by this point you've asked the daughter some clarifying questions, and you understand her core concerns a little better. Since you've kept yourself in a calm state, and have taken in information through observation, you can now reflect, and sort through the data you have. This happens quickly, because your brain is searching for situations like this that have occurred before, that you successfully resolved. Perhaps you're thinking about what other resources you need or contemplating the courses of action at your disposal.

C: Choose

Here's the point where you are able to make a choice of how you are going to respond, based on what you've been able to gather through the previous three steps of Pause, Observe, and Reflect. By remaining calm and open, you've been able to tap into your perspective as well as your knowledge of the situation to choose an ideal response.

H: make it Happen

You've reset yourself so you could effectively pause, observe, reflect and choose the right next step. Now it's time to take action.

YOU MAY FIND yourself naturally or instinctively applying these steps when you have the bandwidth to respond. By bandwidth, I mean the amount of energy you have, or how well you're functioning in that moment. When you feel well-rested, happy, and are able to focus and pay attention, these all feed your bandwidth. Your ability to respond is directly related to your bandwidth and you can clearly see that space between stimulus (what's just happened) and response (how you're dealing with it).

In reaction mode, it can be difficult to suspend time for a few moments and take advantage of that observing space. You can liken it to sitting in the audience and observing, versus being on stage immersed in the drama. In the pause you can see both what's happening, as in gather information and tap into your feelings. You can consider how the clarity and the quality of your thinking is being impacted and then make better choices that will support the outcome you want to create.

Consider this scenario.

There is that one particularly 'passionate family', that as soon as you see them walking down the hall toward you, your heart starts to race, you look down to see if you need to tie your shoes (even though your shoes don't have laces) in order to avoid eye contact and a dreaded conversation. Your ability to respond has been hijacked by the emotional rise in you. Perhaps you had previous experiences with this family and their tone of voice felt condescending. Or you've witnessed them speaking impatiently with one of your co-workers, who you helped to calm down after the family left.

Nothing has even happened with them yet and you are in reaction mode. You have jumped to the conclusion that what's occurred in the past will happen this time, and you just don't have the energy to deal with them right now. Maybe you're run down, feeling depleted for any number of reasons. There is just too much going on at work right now. Sound familiar? Maybe you had a bad start to your morning, and you're focused on getting your residents ready for breakfast. You're feeling behind schedule, and you just had a family member come out of nowhere asking you to come with them right away to help their mom get on the toilet. And you were in the middle of helping another resident with her hair and lipstick.

When we find ourselves in that state of overwhelm or feeling deflated, where the proverbial molehills have become mountains, and we are tempted to wave the white flag of defeat and resignation, taking a few seconds to inhale a deep breath, to slow down and leave the default mode of reaction, can be the first step in doing a *reset*. This cannot happen without a concerted effort though.

The ability to *reset* requires awareness and intention.

YOU NEED to have the awareness, that is, to be able to notice how you're feeling and to understand that how you show up and interact will either help or hinder you and those around you. Returning to the experience of the interaction with a new family on admission day, having an intention can greatly improve your ability to respond, rather than react. You can ask yourself questions like this:

What kind of energy do I want to bring to this new family's admission day?

What kind of a first impression do I want to create?

Connecting through the stress of this day can be trying or transformational for them. So much of the outcome depends on the first moments of interaction, and they set the tone for how things either progress or unravel in the meeting.

Reset Your Energy

CONSIDER two specific areas in your reset strategy. Firstly, think about your energy--the way that you show up and how you bring yourself into a room. Jill Bolte Taylor writes in *My Stroke of Insight*, "I really needed people to take responsibility for the kind of energy they brought me."[1]

In 1996 at the age of 37, Taylor, a Harvard-trained brain scientist, experienced a stroke, which she writes about in her book. In an interview with Oprah, she shared her perspective that there are two kinds of people on the planet. There are those who bring you energy and those who take energy away. As she lay in her hospital bed, recovering from this massive stroke, she recognized that she had a precious reservoir of energy and she needed those who came into her room to bring her energy, not take it away. The last thing she needed was for people to be bringing bad energy into her room. I suspect Taylor had a heightened sensitivity to how other people's energy was impacting her. You may find this interesting, that she also shared in her Oprah interview that the right hemisphere of the brain can perceive those people who are there to help and those who are just showing up.

Have you ever worked with, been friends with, or even worse, are you related to someone that just sucks the life out of you? After spending time with them, you feel drained, or just plain negative and edgy? It's likely that their energy has impacted you. Maybe you've witnessed the reverse where you feel energized and lighter when you've spent time with someone who just radiates positivity and joy?

We have all been in situations where someone comes into the room or meeting, and you can just feel the energy shift or drain in the room. Or maybe you and your spouse are going to a friend's house for dinner, and as soon as you walk into their home you get the sense that they were just arguing with each other, even with the hugs and smiles they give you. Have you been in the situation where you have just walked back to the nurse's station and a couple of your co-workers are standing there but not speaking to you or each other? You don't know what just happened, but it feels tense and uncomfortable?

Your energy impacts others – and if you're bringing in stressed energy from the last conversation or meeting you just had, it will likely have a negative impact.

This is called emotional contagion. How you feel and how you share those feelings, whether consciously or subconsciously, impacts those around you positively or negatively. And the impact is heightened even more if you happen to be in a position of authority. The team is watching how you set the tone for the rest of them.

How you present yourself, and the energy you bring into the room, will affect the quality of the meeting and the conversation. By intentionally *resetting*, you are making a conscious choice to have a positive impact and avoid the risk of coming across as unprepared, flustered or distracted.

There are other benefits of paying attention to how we are feeling and how we are coming across to people. Barbara Frederickson and colleagues created the Broaden and Build theory[2], which states that when we feel positive and happy, we are able to be more flexible and creative at work. Our attention broadens. We are able to take in more, and to contribute and appreciate better. When we are feeling negative or afraid, our attention narrows. We tend to focus solely on the problem at hand and aren't able to expand our perspective and consider other factors that may be at play. It goes back to our hardwiring – when we are in danger, our attention narrows to save our lives. If we are being chased by a rhinoceros, we aren't going to notice the lovely flowers on the path. We are focused on not being trampled and getting out alive!

What this means is this: the more positive and happier you feel will directly influence how creatively you work and engage with those around you.

When we are feeling negative, our focus narrows because our

attention is so committed to the task and its completion that we don't broaden our view to read emotions and cues that would help us build a stronger relationship.

And here's how I think we are negatively impacted when we are feeling run down, stressed, negative. We are less able to manage our emotions, to self-regulate, and that's when we can say something or when an "if looks could kill" moment can set us off, triggering a negative reaction from the other person. Self-regulation and resetting protects and strengthens your bandwidth, giving you choice to manage your emotions, to stabilize yourself so you aren't knocked sideways by someone else's energy.

Having a negative interaction with a family member, because emotions are running high, and both sides end up "going reactive", can ruin the rest of your day. Have you ever, for example, had a run in with a family member, and then the rest of your day seems to be scattered with angry thoughts, what you could have said, what you should have said, and then wonder if you even have the energy to come into work tomorrow and do it all again?

If you could have a do over and rerun that scenario with the insight to reset yourself, practice PORCH, it could be much less stressful and drama-filled, and you could have saved yourself from emotionally bleeding all over the floor.

NEVER underestimate the power of your energy and your presence and how you can impact and influence others!

***

Reset Your Focus

THE SECOND *RESET* opportunity is with your focus. As a culture, we suffer from what is referred to as continuous partial attention, a term coined by Linda Stone in 1998.[3] This is a state where we are always on, paying partial attention, continuously. And even more so today we are continuously 'connected' through our devices. It's like we are in high alert, scanning our environments, in an effort to not miss anything. In our attempt to be 'always accessible' we actually make ourselves inaccessible to the people sitting right in front of us. We are accustomed to being in a state of reaction and distraction. We have all had the experience of feeling unimportant and disappointed when we meet with someone who is distracted. It's about residue again. Unless you are deliberate in the way that you reset yourself, the emotions and thoughts about what was happened in your last interaction, or many previous interactions will be carried with you into everything you do next.

To be present, fully attentive to what is happening in front of you and the needs of the people you are intending to support, you'll need to clear distracting thoughts, emotions and devices.

Reset so that you are able to meet your families where they are by making the space in your head, as well as your heart, to be fully attentive with them. It's possible for family members, and maybe even likely, that when they show up at your seniors' care home, on one of their most difficult days, they are not at their best.

For example, a friend of mine went through the wringer with her dad, who was having falls at home, then was sent to hospital and because he was a 'bed blocker' he was put on the crisis list and within a few weeks was placed into a long-term care home. By the time she and her mom were bringing her father to be admitted, they were at the end of their rope. They felt processed by the system, and also felt like everyone was just passing the buck with his failing health, and quite frankly, they were expecting the same kind of treatment and experience with this last stop in the system. Can you imagine how tense and afraid they must have felt when they walked through those doors? By not resetting and preparing yourself for the meeting with your new resident and family, you could negatively impact the start of that new relationship.

I know for me, after eighteen months of hundreds of

appointments, having my husband Ty on the crisis list while I was trying to balance work, kids and his care, I felt like a cat on a screen just waiting for someone to slam the door shut and send me flying. I was poised on a knife's edge of despair and depletion, and that was before I even walked into the front door. At Ty's admission meeting, I could feel the staff member's distractedness and busyness. I wonder now how differently I could have felt had they taken the time to reset themselves, and to come into that space with us prepared to make a heartfelt connection with us, help us feel a little bit better, and to take just a bit of the sting out of an emotionally draining day.

Here are a few simple ways to *reset:*

- **Take some deep breaths.**

This helps to get you centered and it is a way to literally catch your breath and slow down, creating a sense of grounding or presence. This could be just ten to fifteen seconds to take three deep inhales and exhales, calm your nervous system, slow your heartrate and lower and stabilize your blood pressure. It's a quick and effective way to interrupt your current state with minimal effort. We have to breathe anyway, right?

- **Give yourself a shake.**

Shaking is intrinsic to all animals, including humans, to release the tension that being in fight or flight response brings. For example, a gazelle will shake uncontrollably after being chased by and escaping from a lion to release the stress hormones and adrenaline – and then it will go back to eating grass or whatever gazelles do.

Our chronic stress levels can keep us in a fight or flight state. Shaking is a way to release stress from our muscles, get our circulation going, and relieve anxiety and tension, while giving our thinking minds a bit of a break. In essence, shaking helps us to release any unwanted energy that our body is holding onto and it also relieves tension and stress your body is holding onto.

Think about the tension you hold in your body throughout the day. Notice right now as you're reading this, where you feel tense. Does your jaw feel tight? Are your shoulders pulled up toward your ears, or does your neck feel strained? Some of you spend the majority of your day hunched over a keyboard looking at a screen. Some of you may be more physically active, pushing carts and lifting items, which can also create tension. Shaking is a way to get out of your head and into your body – where all of your stress is stored and to 'shake things up a bit' in your usual daily reactive routine.

- **Self-talk**

You can also *reset* using self-talk. What you say to yourself can be as simple as saying, "Okay, time to reset – you're shifting gears." Research on third person self-talk by Ethan Kross and his fellow authors found that by using third person self-talk – referring to yourself as he/she or by your name – is an almost effortless and immediate strategy for instantly regulating one's emotions.[4] You basically distance yourself and in the process improve your self-regulation, which is your ability to manage disruptive emotions or impulses. Road rage as a good example of a self-regulation deficit!

Let's say you just got off the phone with a family member who you experienced as "reaming you out," and you feel upset, angry or frustrated. Practicing third person self-talk could sound like this:

> "Okay Deb, that was unpleasant, and you've dealt with this before and handled it great. So, put this aside, shake it off, because it's time to meet our new family and I know you want to make them feel warm and welcome on what is a difficult day for them. You

can do it–let's go!" (You may want to do this in a closed office so that your co-workers don't think you've lost it!)

Some other reset suggestions that have come from workshop participants are:

> "I will just take a few minutes and go chat with one of our residents. They remind me that no matter what's going on, sometimes just having a few kind words, a smile and maybe even a laugh and a hug can be so calming and soothing."

> "I sweep the energy residue off my arms – I take my left hand, for example, and brush my right arm from my shoulder right down to my hand – think of it like sweeping water off your arms. It's a way for me to detach myself from whatever was sticking to me. I just get it off me."

I see these as micro-*resets* – something a person can do in a short amount of time—from a few seconds to a few minutes. There are also macro-resets such as these examples offered by workshop participants:

> "After work, my husband and I go for a 45- to 60-minute walk – it gives us a chance to share our events of the day with each other, and to bring it to a close. That way I feel some sense of conclusion and can sleep better at night."

> "Taking a hot bath after a long day is a great way to reset."

> "I reset weekly by planning out my week ahead on Sunday night, and reviewing what I need to get done, what I want to get done, and set aside my free time."

RESET to clear the internal chatter that clutters up your mind, so that you can be fully present and attentive to the person in front of you. *Reset* to manage your emotion so that you can stabilize yourself and not get triggered, which makes us go reactive. Making time for micro and macro *resets* will save you energy and therefore bandwidth, so that you can be more resourceful and engaging with others, and feel more positive and energized.

EYES

THE EMOTION OF OXYTOCIN

 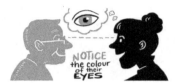

**Sawubona -- a South African greeting which means *I see
you, and by seeing you, I bring you into being***

We've all had this happen. We're having an interaction with someone, like the barista frothing our very expensive latte, or the lone human at the security gate scanning our identification, and they don't even look us in the eye when we're talking to them.

We all do it, don't we?

Think about the last time you were in line ordering a slice of pizza. Did you look up from your phone? Or were you so engrossed in social media, or a video of a cat having cheese tossed on its head that you just said, "pepperoni please, to go" without looking in the staff person's face?

It happens at work too.

What about that moment in the hall yesterday when you were passing Mr. Smith's daughter and she politely asked you if she was going the right way to find her father in the reading room? Did you look up from your tablet? Did you stop scanning your imposing task list long enough to meet her gaze, or did you just give her a "Yep!" and keep walking hurriedly to your office or next task?

You might not have registered how rushed and impersonal that encounter was, (there are so many moments like that in the home during your work day), but she will.

The stakes are higher when the health of a relationship depends on the nature of your contact and connection.

In our transactional world where the task at hand often feels like the highest possible priority to complete in the least amount of time, we can be looking at someone but not really seeing them, not trying to understand them. (And sometimes we don't even look at them).

Being intentional about looking at someone so that they feel seen can be achieved through effective eye contact.

Eye contact is a critical component in trust building. There are some additional body language components, which I'll explain shortly, that reinforce the comfort level of the person we are interacting with.

Let's break down each of these parts.

When we make eye contact, our body releases oxytocin, the trust and bonding hormone, (also called the cuddle hormone). Oxytocin is a 'feel good' chemical that is released in our bodies when we feel a connection with someone. Oxytocin tells the brain that everything is all right. This feel good effect can also contribute to being able to empathize with the other person.

When we make eye contact, we take in a person's facial expression. Our interpretation of their mental state and what emotions they might be feeling is possible from this facial scan. When we are aware of how they are feeling, the opportunity for connection exists. Through this small action of making eye contact, we show someone that we are attentive to and interested in them, and in response they are more likely to be interested in interacting with us in a meaningful way.

As we are becoming a culture comprised of people that spend an increasing amount of time looking down at our computers and phones, the act of making eye contact is even more effective at signaling personal interest by contrast and is quickly becoming a differentiator in how others can experience us. Eye contact with another person is a pathway to building trust; it fosters connection.

Body language experts share that to be facing and in front of the other person -- positioned with your heart facing their heart, signals an openness and creates a shared space between you. When you make the effort to openly face the other person, you are being intentional with your presence and your attention. Noticing how you're standing, and your body position relative to whomever you're speaking with, puts you in that moment, right now. Making the adjustment trains your focus on this conversation.

Keeping your hands visible is the third component of this strategy. When someone can see your hands, their subconscious, which is constantly looking for danger, settles into ease. This goes back to our hardwired-for-survival brains, so even though it's highly unlikely the person poses a physical threat, your subconscious is scanning for danger.

Body language expert Mark Bowden[1] writes, "Your audience's instinctual 'reptilian' brain and emotional 'limbic' brain need to see your body to decide what they think your intentions and feelings are towards them. The less you show, the more they make those feelings and intentions up, and tend to default towards the negative."

So why not take that subconscious concern off the table by showing your hands – and not in a jazz-hands kind of way!

A really simple way to ensure you are making eye contact:

Notice the colour of the other person's eyes.

When I'm facilitating workshops, I often take people through the exercise where I invite participants to turn to the person next to them and notice the colour of their eyes. As they turn to look at the other person and really look to see the colour of their eyes, conversation erupts, and I regularly hear rumblings of nervous laughter.

Here are some of the actual comments I've heard:

"I was amazed that I never noticed the colour of their eyes before, and we've worked together for years."

"It actually felt uncomfortable at first to be told to look into the eyes of the person sitting next to me. Once I did, I felt like I had to talk to them to break the awkwardness. We both started laughing."

"Once we got over the discomfort, it felt really nice to actually take a few moments and SEE the other person. It's remarkable what you can see when you block out the distraction and discomfort and just connect with each other."

I wonder if the release of oxytocin in these workshops is the reason people start talking and laughing every time I suggest this exercise – they've just experienced a feel good boost of energy just by noticing the colour of someone else's eyes for a few seconds.

Let me note here however, that there are cultures where this kind of eye contact is not appropriate, so I'm not suggesting you apply this unless you are certain of its propriety. Cultural competency – and being able to respect the culture you are participating in, is a critical foundation for being in an empathetic experience.

If while reading this, there's another human – or even a pet close by, put the book down, and go over to them and really look at the colour of their eyes. Notice how it feels to be so intentional. Ask them how it felt to be looked at that way, (assuming they can talk and not just bark or meow).

When we make the time and intention to notice a person's eye colour, it has the effect of slowing us down for just a moment. It can get us out of our head and focused on someone else.

I've begun practicing this when I'm giving my coffee order and I repeatedly notice how the server is immediately aware that I'm making eye contact with them. The way they look back at me sometimes makes me wonder if I have something stuck to my face, because they return a more intense look. They seem surprised that I'm trying to do this, that I'm intentionally interacting with them, instead of busying my gaze (which is obviously the norm) by scanning the gift cards and snacks positioned in front of the cash register for just the purpose of stealing our attentiveness. I know how difficult this can feel, even three seconds is a long time with intentional eye contact, yet the energy boost that both of us can get from this little interaction is remarkable.

I also find that when I'm making eye contact, I feel respectful of the other person's time and attention. I'm showing appreciation for their presence and by bringing energy to our connection, simply connecting with them through eye contact, I'm showing that I'm interested in them.

Isn't it amazing how much we can be communicating with someone simply by making eye contact?

Our nervous system relaxes when we fix eye contact and we can be more responsive and receptive. A brain that is not preoccupied with assessing danger or inspecting the body language of others is free to make more connections. This is how your best listening and assimilating of information can happen. You can't do your best thinking or take in everything a person is saying to you if, while you're listening, you're also making a mental grocery list. Thinking of things causes shifts in eye movements that others can notice. Noticing a person's eye colour focuses our brains and we hear and understand more.

Eye contact is a conduit for your energy and emotions. It's simple and it works.

My mom was living in assisted living for about two years, and we had recently moved her to the memory care floor. Even though we are current customers/family in this home, she is a new resident and we are a new family within this area of the home.

On a day I was leaving my mom after a concerning visit, I approached one of the nurses who was working away at her med cart in the hallway. I introduced myself as Carol's daughter and let her know that my mom seemed extremely lethargic and I was concerned about her. She glanced over at me, then back at the meds she was sorting or doing something with and told me that she was the one to take care of her this morning and that she was fine. I was standing there, almost in disbelief that I was being brushed off like that. This was the first time we were meeting each other, and I was getting a transactional conversation. The first impression she was leaving me with was that she was too busy to stop what she was doing to look at me, listen to what I wanted to share, and to have a healthy dialogue about my concerns.

The exchange was probably not more than thirty seconds long, and perhaps she had no idea how her lack of eye contact and interest impacted me. And yet, it wouldn't have taken much more time to put down what she was doing (or even let me know she was in the middle of something and needed to complete it before she could chat with me), to turn her body so that her heart was facing my heart, and to make eye contact while I shared what was bothering me that morning.

We all have an innate desire to feel these things when we are spending time and communicating with those around us.

In our transactional world, where our exchanges can too often have a procedural quality, we are experiencing a relational deficit.

We humans are social beings that are stimulated by relational interactions that foster the natural development of bonds of connection. In our commodified, consumer culture we have allowed the fast pace and the drive for results to normalize this transactional type of encounter with one another.

In her article "Stop Googling. Let's Talk," MIT professor Sherry Turkle looks at the impact of being 'always connected' and how it is eroding our ability to be relational with the people sitting right in front of us. Turkle writes "But it is in this type of conversation - where we learn to make eye contact, to become aware of another person's posture and tone, to comfort one another and respectfully challenge one another - that empathy and intimacy flourish. In these conversations, we learn who we are."[2] This is more likely to happen when we don't have our phones in front of us, stealing our attention from the person across the table. Phones are not the only way to be distracted though, and I'm not suggesting that you have yours in front of you at work. It is possible to look right at someone but be so focused on processing your thoughts that you're not really seeing them, or even hearing them for that matter.

Focus opens up the opportunity to gain knowledge.

Consider the last time you had a really useful and productive conversation at work where the interruptions were controlled, and the distractions managed. In addition to the work that got done, what did you learn about that person? What insight did you gain about their concerns or challenges? How were you able to think and reflect about what needed to happen next?

Let me give you an example from my work in a shadowing session where I was silently present during a staff member's work day.

A resident's family was expressing that their concerns weren't being addressed in a timely manner, after many conversations with the care staff on the floor. As you know, on the floor, especially near the nurse's station, there is a constant buzz of noise and activity. The family members shared how much they appreciated management pulling the team together and arranging a meeting with their family in one of the home's meeting rooms. Even though that family had shared the same concerns and feedback 'on the floor' with the staff, in this more controlled setting, they had everyone's full attention without distractions and interruptions, and people could actually finish their thoughts and collaborate on solutions. The gathered group was enthusiastic and committed to leaning into each other's worlds to ensure better outcomes for this family and their loved one's care and contentment.

Think about all of the various interactions, or transactions you have on any given day, like sitting in a reception area waiting for an appointment. How many people (including you) are sitting there looking at their devices or reading magazines? When you check in, does the receptionist actually look at you, or are his or her eyes scanning a computer screen rather than acknowledging you standing in front of them?

When I think back to all of the hundreds of medical appointments I took my husband Ty to, I realize they mostly felt like a business transaction. On the rare occasion that a staff person took a few seconds to look at my face and make eye contact, to just slow down and meet me where I was in that moment, it felt unusual, and like a breath of fresh air that I desperately needed. I felt seen, like our presence had been witnessed and that we mattered. There was an empathetic energy, like a nudge of reassurance that they would do their best to help us.

The Effort to Engage

BEING intentional about your body position can have a positive impact. Earlier, I discussed how effective it can be, just to be attentive to how you position relative to the other person. Douglas Stone and Sheila Heen write about "leaky body language" in their book *Thanks for the Feedback*.[3] They describe how faces and tones can be leaky. The only person who can't see your face is you. And so our face becomes our own blind spot. We can be leaking how we really feel by our facial expression, or we can also leak out unintended signals based on how other people are perceiving our facial expression

Other than when you look into a mirror, or see yourself in photos, when you are with other people, they can all see your face and expressions and you can't, and they are getting clues about what you're thinking and feeling. These clues leak out, showing even though we don't always want them to, with micro expressions. How we are truly feeling can show on our face – and people react to the subtle nuances in our eyes, and facial expressions that convey mood and attitude.

We are sometimes unaware of the messages our faces send.

"RESTING BITCH FACE" is a popular term these days, referencing how our face looks when we are passive, or resting, or just listening. Think about how your face may look to an observer while you sit watching television or listening to a speaker. You can't see what your facial expression is, and you're not focused on how you might appear while in your 'resting state'. Even though you may be intently focused on what's being said, the other person observes an expression that looks grumpy, disinterested or "bitch-faced". What your face is communicating may be nothing like what you're actually feeling in that moment.

For those of you who have kids, have you ever experienced that 'I'm not listening to you' face as you ask them how their day is? That's exactly what I'm talking about—their faces tell us exactly how they feel, and we have no difficulty reading it.

Now, consider this in a situation at work. You may be deep in thought, and someone approaches you with a question. As you look at them, it's quite possible you're still thinking about what you were just working on, and the look on your face reflects that you aren't fully attentive to what they are saying. They will react to that leak. They can't know the importance of what you were just working on, and they are trying to read you through your face and body language as they engage you in conversation. If you have a facial expression that communicates disinterest, or what the other person perceives as a 'mood', they might react with defensiveness. Reactions that are prompted by mistaken assumptions can only lead to problems down the road.

Studies show that 93% of our communication is non-verbal–only 7% is our words. The remainder is our tone, presence, body language, and facial expressions.

You know the saying--it's not what you say, it's how you say it. This is where 'leaky tones' play a role in communication. How you say something impacts what other people believe you mean to infer with the tone you use.

Body language reflects how we feel, offering the intention behind our words.

In my consulting work, families have shared with me that in non-critical situations when there is a problem, how the staff react to their concern is usually more upsetting than the issue itself. Family members tell me that they hesitate to initiate even a quick inquiry because they feel they are imposing on the staff member's time. Families really do understand how busy staff are. A family member has told me that they felt like it was difficult to keep a staff member's attention because of all the comings and goings on the floor. I've even had family members share that it seems the staff's eyes are 'glazing over' while sharing a concern about their loved one.

I think each of us can put ourselves in their shoes. Their cherished family member, for whom they take their responsibility as advocate very seriously, lives in that home. They feel strongly that a concern needs to be raised and upon approaching a staff member, they sometimes perceive that a 'glazed over', inattentive or even bored reaction from staff is what they get back. The family members must feel a mix of unresolvable emotions.

And it isn't just one sided, either. I've had staff tell me that sometimes families don't even make eye contact with them, and that makes them feel 'less than', unappreciated and disrespected. Something as simple yet powerful as eye contact, a smile, and acknowledging the other person goes a long way to building trust and respect in the relationship.

The way we appear to be reacting to someone may be even more important than the words being exchanged. This is all within our control. We are capable of choosing to be more relational with people.

Let me share an example from my personal experience. When one particular nurse comes into my mom's assisted living room to administer her medication, he approaches her gently and almost always gets her to smile with a warm touch to her shoulder. He then kneels down to be eye level because she is seated in her wheelchair.

My mom has a quick wit and when he's able to keep up with her, they share a laugh – a relational connection. She feels the energy he brings to the room. She's not feeling handled or managed, she's feeling respected, appreciated and well cared for.

In a more transactional scenario, the nurse would come in and be solely focused on getting the medication into my mom as quickly as possible, so that he could get back to inputting information and moving on to the next resident. The personal connection and subtle attempts to engage with her would be missing, and my mother would feel processed, and perhaps begin to react negatively to having her medication administered.

Connecting through eye contact and body language are ways to leverage the power of your presence, and making use of them as you interact with people doesn't need to take any more time. Just be mindful enough to get out of your head, drop down into your heart and seek connection through your physical presence and be empathetic and relational.

CURIOSITY

THE QUESTION CONNECTION

Empathy starts when we become curious about that person's journey and experiences.

Curiosity is about seeking knowledge and wanting to know about something. Curiosity has value in supporting your thinking, plays a role in how you relate to others, and in how you can influence outcomes. Being curious could help you live longer and could even enhance your mental health. Being curious – having the desire for information -- actually shifts the energy that you are feeling and projecting to others. Curiosity is an antidote to a fixed mindset and a gateway to empathy.

There are many benefits to developing your curiosity mindset including a lower mortality rate[1], higher self-esteem[2] and greater life satisfaction.[3]

I know that on first mention, you might not see how curiosity plays a role in your work, or in your ability to enjoy relating with others at work. But I assure you, from the first interaction, when you meet new residents and families, curiosity is something that can really shift the tone of how you relate.

Let's consider how things could go right from the admissions meeting point on.

At the typical move-in day meeting questions are asked based on a standardized checklist, according to procedure. Your new families are walking into an admissions day after having packed up their loved one to get them to the home for what could be a half day or even full day experience, depending on how much activity needs to happen. For some, that day was preceded by months working through the long-term care bed approval process, an arduous and transactional one where more significant medical needs moves a person higher on the waiting list or onto the crisis list.

A heart wrenching decision and life change is being overlaid with a transactional approach to the need for analysis and review based on all the objective and subjective data contained in that file. The emotional strain of wading through the approval process, documenting physical and cognitive decline while accepting that care by family is no longer sufficient or safe, has taken its toll on families before they enter the home on admission day. No wonder it's an emotionally draining day! And yet it can feel like an 'emotional compromise'. There is the volume of transactions that are needed, and for good reason. Staff need to know as much as they can about the resident in order to keep them safe and manage this transition without any hiccups in the care protocol. But there is also this sad reality of uprooting someone and placing them in an institutional setting – sharing living, dining, and entertainment spaces with a lot of other people who also need this level of care.

When I was on the family member side of the table at our admissions day for my husband, the story I told earlier, I felt like no one was really curious about us — as a couple, as a family, as human beings. They proceeded down the checklist of questions and we responded. In retrospect, with just a few simple questions, they could have learned so much about us and that information would have given them insight, helped them relate to Ty as their incoming resident and to me as their new and stressed-out family member. As much as I was consumed with the angst of this move, I was also thinking about our kids, who were nineteen and fourteen when their dad was moving into long-term care – something that none of their peer group could even relate to. I know it would have made us feel more welcomed. It could also have helped us feel a bit more comfortable as the reality that we were becoming a part of their community was unfolding.

Hey, I understand the challenge of this, adding on tasks when there are time constraints and you need to move on to other to-do's, it's a struggle. I also know that for staff in the home, the resident is the priority, but also getting to know the family will add to supporting the resident as well as your staff now and in the future.

Both you and the families enter the admission meeting with something that the other person needs. You have new family members coming into your home – a place you know like the back of your hand – and this is all new for them. They are coming onto your 'turf', your workplace, where your level of comfort is high, and theirs is likely very low. The family knows their loved one best, and in most cases their health care needs and preferences very well. Another knowledge gap exists too. You know what is going to occur today and in the coming days and they cannot foresee because this is likely the first and perhaps only time this person is going to have the identity and role of a resident's family member.

Prior to the admissions meeting, the resident was a name in a file, mostly described by diagnosis and behaviours. You have some basic facts about the family – spouse, kids, siblings – the who's who. Someone in your home has likely spoken with one of the family members to coordinate the paperwork prior to the admission, or to have them come in and see the room and verbally accept, but that may be the extent of contact to that point. The family sitting before you is walking into the unknown. Put yourself in their seats, if you can. Think of what this experience is like for them. How you address them, relate to them, even how you try to build a relationship with them in future could be improved by following curiosity in this private setting.

Questions reveal your interest and curiosity. Consider what have they experienced medically prior to admission here. (I'm not talking just about procedures or diagnosis, I'm talking about their experiences with the health care system and the lingering impressions they have about those interactions).

- How are they feeling about this 'final step' with their loved one?
- What are they worrying about?
- What is important to them?

When we are genuinely curious, we are in a state of not knowing and have a genuine interest to learn.

The other person can be the bridge, providing insight, reflections and responses to our questions — it's an opportunity to build a relationship through conversation and discovery.

I think the secret sauce to being truly curious is a balance of enquiry — asking questions — and listening with the intent to hear not only what's being said, but what's not being said — what's being felt. Listening generously and in a meaningful way will bring the kind of understanding from which a relationship can grow.

Imagine how much energy and time can be saved by stepping back and being curious enough to want to find a better way to bring this family and their loved one into the home on the first day?

I had an experience with a family I was shadowing that is a useful illustration. I was speaking with the daughter whose mother became a resident three months before. Mary described to me that her mother had dementia, spoke very little English, and was refusing baths. Mary believed that in her mother's mind, she was a single 22-year-old woman and didn't understand why strangers wanted to take her clothes off and put her into a bath. Mary's routine was to come to the home three or four times a week and she told me that she was feeling like she needed to take the lead to help the staff with giving her mom have a bath. "But," she said, "surely this isn't the first time they've had a resident refusing baths?" Mary was frustrated that she needed to visit her mother whenever a bath was scheduled. That is what was happening. What was not happening was a sit-down, brainstorming session with the family and staff to get curious about how they could change their approach with Mary's mother.

Curiosity begins with questions. What could they try? What was working when the daughter cared for her mother in their own home? What could be contributing to her mother's refusal? Is she afraid? Is she cold? Is she embarrassed? The only way to find out, and the only way to improve the comfort for Mary's mother is for everyone involved in her care to get curious and have an intentional conversation with a desire to learn and try a new way.

When you have an angry or upset family member, choosing curiosity as a response can create a pathway to resolution.

When we are facing potential conflict, our natural instinct is the fight or flight mindset. When our fight or flight is triggered, we are in a reactive state and just looking to protect ourselves by standing our ground or escaping. We can go into a fight mode and get defensive which could mean getting into an argument, because we can get judgmental and self-protective. When we go into flight mode, we do whatever we can to remove ourselves from the conflict, by simply not addressing the issue, or deferring to management in an attempt to deflect or buy time.

In the spirit of 'standing our ground' we may be so focused on our position, that we aren't able to see the other person's perspective because we are so busy justifying, defending or trying to give them answers we think they want to hear. This can deepen the rift between us. We can't connect with them when we are solidly rooted in our version of what happened, more than trying to gain an understanding of theirs.

There are three emotional states that curiosity can help to cancel out by reducing friction and stress.

Curiosity cancels out the tendency to make assumptions.

HUMANS JUMP TO CONCLUSIONS. We are hardwired to assemble assumptions to make sense of things. This is the doubled-edged sword of experience. We jump into our memory banks of similar situations, pull out what's worked before, (assuming they're pretty comparable), and predict what might happen this time.

Have you found yourself listening to a co-worker or a family member and thinking to yourself, I know where THIS is going. You've locked yourself into an assumption because something about this story feels like a repeat from another experience. Sometimes our assumption is correct, but what about when it's wrong?

Our natural human behaviour is to seek evidence that supports our position. We like to be right and we seek out evidence that supports us being right. We naturally filter out pieces of data that contradict our belief and notice data that supports our belief.

Let's say for example you have a family member that you experience as a "complainer". You may feel like no matter what you do it is never good enough for this family. You feel they are high maintenance and difficult to deal with. What likely happens is that any time you see them you assume that they will be difficult and cause frustration for you. What could happen is that even if they have a reasonable question or request, you can interpret it as them 'being difficult as usual' because that's what your brain is scanning for. Similarly, if a family perceives that a staff member is 'just doing this job because they have to', even when this staff member wants to help the family by sharing feedback or an update about the resident, the family may not see or appreciate this communication's intention. We make up our minds and then filter out any evidence that doesn't support our position.

What if we allowed for curiosity instead of assumption?

When we become curious, when we try to understand, we are opening ourselves up to seeing and better appreciating the other person's perspective based on their view point and experience.

And when we are curious, we are much more receptive, we soften our presence, because we are shifting out of the mindset of needing to have all the answers because we think others expect us to, particularly as leaders - and become more comfortable with a level of not knowing. This creates a sense of vulnerability and with that softening comes an invitation for connection. Being curious invites contribution from others, because the behaviours that accompany curiosity are listening and asking questions.

When we are listening with the intention to understand and connect, we put our own agenda aside, along with our assumption, and maybe even that desire to jump into action because we don't yet have the full picture.

Curiosity cancels out anger.

When we are curious, it's very difficult (if not impossible) to be angry. Curiosity softens us and renders us receptive, making a more productive and positive conversation possible. Think about it. When we are feeling angry with someone, it's usually because we are so committed to our emotion-driven opinion. Test this for yourself. Next time you feel angry, about someone else's reaction or behaviour, consider what it is specifically that you're angry about. Then ask yourself questions such as:

- I wonder what's going on with them to behave like that?
- I wonder if that was their intention?
- What am I missing here that could help me better understand what's going on?
- Is it possible they aren't actually trying to make me mad?
- What's triggered in me to create this reaction?

Let's face it – when we make assumptions, they are just stories we are creating in our minds. They may be right, or they may be wrong. And sometimes, the stories we are creating prompt our behaviour and affect our attitudes and moods. We can get angry without all of the evidence.

Even though we know cognitively that we're not capable of reading other people's minds, we believe based on our past experience and observations that we have them all figured out. We think we know what others are thinking or feeling.

And here's something else to consider. Moods are usually the cause and not the result of our problem. So when we are in a negative mood, it influences what we are actually paying attention to. Our internal state – let's say anger – then triggers our reaction to the situation. By bringing curiosity into reflective thinking, you could possibly uncover that your mood is influencing your reaction, rather than the behaviour of the person you are reacting to.

Curiosity cancels out judgment.

The third emotional state that curiosity can cancel out is being judgmental. Being curious can create compassion, whereas being judgmental usually feels, well, judgey! But – as humans we are actually programmed to judge other people's behaviours as a way to save our time and energy for more important things. It is within our core brain behaviour to quickly size up situations and people. But if we don't know what is motivating people, we won't know how to react. The best response, one which allows for the best possible outcome, is to withhold judgment. Developing your curiosity takes practice and consistency.

I want to clarify that there is a distinction between having judgment and being judgmental. It is important to have 'sound judgment' – it's a significant leadership attribute – to discern and assess to make good decisions. A critical part of your job is to use sound decision-making, as it relates to your resident's care and well-being. You also need to have good judgment with how you relate to families and the way you respond to concerns they raise. You use that judgment when you share updates that may be difficult for the families to hear and you choose what's most relevant or important to share.

Judgment is defined as:

"the ability to judge, make a decision, or form an opinion objectively, authoritatively, and wisely, especially in matters affecting action; good sense; discretion." However, being judgmental is different and defined as: "Having or displaying an extremely critical point of view or tending to judge people too quickly and critically".[4]

Maintain good judgment without being judgmental.

Here's an example. Let's say a family member is complaining that their loved one's brief isn't being changed enough during the day. It would be tempting to get judgmental about the family, thinking "they have no idea the level of care we ARE providing," or "we ARE changing them as per the care plan, these people are just over the top and unreasonable."

Having sound judgment in this example could involve:

- Clarifying the family's concern by taking the time to have them explain what they perceive as the 'reality' of the situation. What's causing them to have this concern? Can they provide examples of what their concern is? What facts, observations or assumptions are driving their concern? Take the time to hear what they are upset about.
- Sharing factual information about the care you are providing. Perhaps you could refer to the care plan and what standard was agreed upon when it was created. Or you might share the documentation to reflect the schedule the staff are following.
- Determine an agreed upon approach that is doable for the staff and that addresses the family's need.

The fact that you are being curious and asking questions from a healthy place of curiosity can build on that sense of a person being seen AND being heard!

**Curiosity can be a bridge to
compassion and empathy.**

Think of it as practicing compassionate curiosity. In a state of compassionate curiosity, we can better understand how other people's emotions, their feelings of loss of control and their guilt may be impacting their thoughts and their behaviours. When we can appreciate someone else's circumstances, the journey they've been on, and meet them where they are, without judgment, connection is possible.

There are two things that we attribute other people's behaviour to: their situation and their personality. When we make situational attributions, we believe their behaviour is due to something in their situation. For example, our co-worker might have been short with us, and we assume it is because he or she is tired or overworked. Personality attributions are about the person's character. When we make these attributions, we believe their behaviour has something to do with their personality. Assuming that same co-worker who was short with us is an impatient or unkind person would be a personality attribution. Personality attributions are more enduring and long-lasting. Being impatient or unkind is a consistent way of being, compared to being tired or overworked, which may be temporary. What you attribute people's behaviour to will predict how long this impression of them stays with you, and curiosity will support you in arriving at a more likely understanding about what's contributing to their behaviour. In other words, understanding why they are acting as they are.

Coming back to the context of the admissions meeting, I think it is important to resist the urge to be a firehose of information. You may know the admissions process so well, or think you need to be the expert and have all the answers, but chances are the family isn't going to remember all of those details. As I mentioned earlier, what they will remember, for a very long time though, is how they felt during the admissions meeting. Remember Maya Angelou's quote — people will never forget how you made them feel.

Being curious is a helpful approach when you're dealing with any challenging situation, but especially when you are facing a 'passionate' family member. Asking questions and showing genuine interest in finding clarity can slow the conversation down, help de-escalate emotions and ideally prevent you from becoming reactive or defensive.

For you, being curious can cancel out assumptions, anger or judgment that could lead you toward incorrect conclusions, and result in the family not feeling heard or feeling misunderstood, and potentially causing irreparable damage to the relationship. No one wants that to happen. Curiosity draws us away from our inflexible mindset, the view that things will turn out as they always have, and where we can only see what is not working and won't be helpful. Flexibility in mindset is a more productive place for people to interact because it holds open the possibility of a compromise. While you are asking questions, both you and the family are reframing your presumptions about one another, shifting the emotional state through a more comfortable, slower exchange. You may both find that your thinking was not based on fact when you reflect.

Reivich and Shatte write about "thinking traps", our habitual ways of thinking that stop us from a having a more flexible and accurate way of thinking.[5] We jump to conclusions without evidence. We personalize people's reactions when they have nothing to do with us. We think that we know what others are thinking. There is a simple solution to each and all of these traps—

Be curious and ask for clarification.

You can probably think of times when you might have overreacted to a situation; when you went "reactive". It happens to all of us. If you choose to become curious, you can circumvent these reactions and make time for a response that nurtures relationship. This feels better for everyone.

INTENTION

DESIGN OVER DEFAULT

"You cannot get through a single day without having an impact on the world around you. What you do makes a difference, and you have to decide what kind of difference you want to make."[1]

— JANE GOODALL

Y ou have probably noticed in previous chapters, that I have talked about the importance of being intentional – whether it's noticing the need to RESET, make EYE contact or position your body to be more open, and even being intentional with bringing CURIOSITY into conversations. Intention is one of those threads that weaves through the RECIPE, and the focus of this chapter is to do a deeper dive into, well, being intentional with intention.

How often have you found yourself at the end of the day, reflecting on how quickly you cycled through all of the transactions and to-do's that never seem to end, wondering if you made a difference with anything you did?

If someone asked you, "What was the highlight of your day?" would you be able to answer right away? Sometimes it's hard even to remember what you had for breakfast, right?

As we get into the rhythm and routine of our daily lives, we have a natural tendency to operate on auto pilot. According to a study by Daniel Gilbert (who wrote *Stumbling on Happiness*) and Matthew Killingsworth[2] most of us are mentally checked out, running on auto pilot just less than half the time. In this state we find ourselves engaging in the same repetitive habits. Behaving habitually and predictably, it's no wonder that some days feel like we're in the movie "Ground Hog Day," starring Bill Murray, where he is caught in a time loop, repeatedly living the same day over and over.

The more we stay in auto pilot mode, the less happy we actually become. As much as some of us need structure and routine, we also crave novelty and newness. Auto pilot is the path of least resistance, and if we are tired, stressed, or pre-occupied with our own internal chatter, then jumping on the auto pilot bus feels easier because there we don't have to expend too much energy thinking about what we are doing, or why we are doing it. We just do it. We show up but we are not fully present.

But the choice of how you want to present yourself is always yours. You can intentionally shift the nature of your interactions, and as a result, the outcome. The easiest way to clarify is by asking yourself: "What is my intention?"

Ask yourself this very simple question as you work throughout your day and interact with others. It short circuits the tendency to react. As I was preparing a workshop on the contents of this book, I had an experience that brought this concept to life for me, and one that was a great example of the power of clear intentions.

One evening after a long work day, I retrieved a voicemail from my mother's assisted living home. My mom's care needs were increasing, and I was feeling the pressure of being the primary family caregiver and advocate. I was also playing the story in my head that I was taking on the majority of the tasks and 'burden' of caregiving - something that I was all too familiar with, after the seven years of caregiving with my husband.

I sat down at my computer and started typing out an email to my two older brothers. As I typed I could hear my whininess, evidence of the victim mentality was on the screen. Fortunately, I had enough self-awareness to catch myself. I stopped typing and asked myself, "What is my intention with this email? Is it to make them feel bad, guilt trip them because I'm doing all of the heavy lifting?" What outcome could this create in our relationship? While I might have felt validated for a few minutes, it was just as likely I would have felt bad, or embarrassed about my tone and my intention. I rewrote the email with an adjusted intention, which was to provide an update on our mom, and to ask them for help. I was specific about my needs and hit send. Both my brothers responded with gratitude for what I was doing, and assurance that they could absolutely help me out.

If I hadn't stalled my initial reactive thinking and typing with this reflective RESET question "What is my intention"? it could have created unnecessary conflict.

How many times have you found yourself reacting – or snapping, and then regretting what you said or what you did once you had clarity of thought back? For any of us who are parents, we could probably think of at least 6,000 times when we felt like some unknown entity was taking over our minds and our mouths!

- What is my intention?
- How do I want to respond to this?
- What is the best next step?
- What do I want to make happen here?
- How do I want to show up?

These are all great questions to ask yourself before you have any kind of interaction. They pull your focus back a little so that you can observe what is unfolding (or unravelling) with some objectivity. This distance enables you to reset your intention and aim toward your desired outcome.

When you think about your interaction with residents, for example, perhaps you set the intention to share a smile and a laugh as you get the 'transactional' part of your job done. Or when you see a family member, your intention could be to ask them how their day is going, and to really listen with both your attention and body language, so that you are fully present with them, and they feel and see your genuine interest.

Can you imagine what that could create in your relationships?

According to Gilbert and Killingsworth's research, one of the activities that made people the happiest was conversation. Think about how many times a day you engage in conversation – and knowing that engaging in conversation is a pathway to making us happy, why not be intentional about it?

It takes intention to be intentional.

This isn't just something I talk about in the book, I use these techniques myself in my *Family Matters™ program*, when I facilitate family focus groups and take people through an emotion mapping exercise to reflect on their experience with their loved ones' admission into long-term care. I have them share what they were feeling during specific 'moments' in the admission process, from the phone call confirming a bed is available right through to three months after move in day. Before starting the session, I take a moment to reset my energy and my focus, and to ask myself: What is my intention? It can be very emotional for the families, as well as cathartic for them, and the mapping process is significant for us as we work on redesigning the home's admissions process to create better outcomes for families and staff.

My intention is to create an environment of openness and support amongst the family members. I also intend to hear their stories, empathize with their emotions, and acknowledge their courage and the compassion they express for their loved one and the staff at the home. What emerges are memories and feelings that they may have buried away that they are able to now reconcile and recognize as natural parts of this difficult journey.

How about asking yourself this: What kind of first impression do I want to make?

You'll be leaving a first impression regardless, so why not embrace the opportunity, engage with intention, and have a major positive impact? When it comes to first impressions, these family members have no previous experience to base their perception of you on. You have a clean slate to influence how they feel about you. You have the ability and privilege to impact your new family and set the tone for their future relationship with you and your team, on a day that is likely a tough one for them. You can transform this admissions day from being 'a step in the process' into an event where the family members feel your intention and desire to help and support. You have the power to facilitate an outstanding first impression. You can approach the admissions day experience as a pathway to building trust, connection and a relationship with your families.

If you're in a management or leadership position, you have even more eyes watching you. So, if you know you are creating an impression with your presence, why not be thoughtful and intentional with choosing how you want to show up?

Let's go back to our admissions experience, as well as those first few weeks when I was a new family member, trying to get familiar with this 'new normal' of visiting regularly. I had many first impressions with various staff on different shifts, and how those interactions made me feel impacted how I was processing this major life curve ball thrown at us. Of course, you can't take away the guilt, pain, sadness, frustration and angst that families may feel, but you sure can help ease some of it with compassionate connection and empathy. It can be as simple as a smile and a nod, to a 'how are YOU doing' to sharing a quick little update on something positive that happened that day.

———

HERE ARE some questions that you and your team can use to both *reset* and set your intention for family meetings. I truly believe had the team asked themselves these questions and set their intention, it would have been an entirely different admissions experience for Ty and I, and a strong relational foundation could have been set.

- How do I want our new family to feel about and remember this day?
- How can I redesign this transaction into a relational experience?
- How can I adjust my energy so they feel seen, heard, and appreciated?
- If I'm being honest with myself, my default state can sometimes look like...
- If I resist my default of busy, how might it benefit the family? And me?

PRESENT

HONOURING THE SPACE

There is power in your presence.

Today's society programs us to have stunted attention spans. There are a number of studies done, the conflicting results of which state that the average human attention span has dropped from 12 seconds in 2000 to 8 seconds in 2013, (less than the attention span of a goldfish at 9 seconds) and also that attention span is being more impacted by the task itself. Even if you're skeptical that the attention span of a goldfish can be measured, (yes, the study actually compares humans to goldfish), I think we can agree that the distracted, rushed, and reactive way we live has severely impacted our ability to be fully attentive, present and focused.

Being present is a concept in common parlance these days. By present, in the RECIPE for Empathy I mean being aware of and paying attention to where you are, who you're with and what you are doing in that very moment.

How can we be creating experiences that we savour if we're not actually being attentive when they are happening?

JUST THIS MORNING I was listening to a 4:06-minute guided meditation,[1] when these words really resonated with me..."Looking for a little calm in the chaos? Sharpen your brain's ability to concentrate, focus on a task and manage distractions with this meditation." I sat down, turned on the meditation, my dog jumped up on my lap with his stuffed giraffe in his mouth, (making sounds that only pugs can make with a straight face), and I began anyway. It was practical and powerful. Only 4:06 minutes long - because after all, I had things to do and that was all the time I could afford, I told myself. And yet, it guided me to be in the moment. The meditation host invited me to notice any sounds, to be aware of how the air felt on my skin. She reminded me to pay attention to my breath - through my nostrils, or in my chest. She talked me through the slowing down, the noticing and the awareness. What I appreciated the most was the reminder that it's okay (and quite normal) to have my thoughts drift off, and her tip that just noticing my thoughts drifting is progress. In fact, it's actually a good thing, because I can practice bringing my focus back to 'the breath' and regain presence. It's like a meditation muscle that is strengthening my brain.

It can be difficult to just stop and breathe when you have a day full of tasks and responsibilities. I know how it goes -- you think you'll make time at the end of the day, when surely there will be a moment to breathe, right?

What if you think of presence like giving your nervous system a time out – a reprieve from the onslaught of stress and stimulation. When we are practicing being present, we aren't focused on the past or unresolved issues, nor are we directing our attention to the future, and whatever we haven't yet experienced or made happen. You've heard this a million times. This may sound like one of those Instagram platitudes, but there's good sense in this sentiment.

The only time we have right now is the present, and how we show up is laying the foundation for what comes next.

I know how daunting it sounds to have yet another detail to add to the way you conduct your day. Let me tell you why it's worth your time and energy to practice presence for your own health and well-being, and how strengthening your ability to be present creates positive outcomes with others.

While writing this book I battled with distractions impacting my focus and attention. I had been trained in twenty-plus years in a corporate atmosphere that multi-tasking was not only a strength, it was a necessity. My last office actually had two doors - one that accessed the human resources department and another that went to the executive area. Unless I was having a private meeting, I liked having both doors open. And with open doors come a lot of interaction, (which could be viewed as disruptions and distractions). Those interactions were part of my job, but their frequency trained me to be "on" and "ready to react" when a problem walked through the door. As part of a casual experiment, I timed how long I was able to work on my own before someone required my attention. It ranged anywhere from two minutes to six minutes. I became accustomed to frequent and regular shifts in my attention, and I suspect you experience a similar cadence in your work life. Think about how many interactions you have on any given day, that are not of your initiation, with residents, families, co-workers, managers, vendors, and whatever technology you use for business and personal record keeping and communication...and that's just during your work day!

During the writing of the **RECIPE for Empathy** I needed some attention reinforcement. I used the Pomodoro Technique (developed by Francesco Cirillo)[2] which is essentially this: work in twenty-five-minute intervals, with a short break in between. Rather than using my home office to write (where I could look out onto the street and be distracted by anything that moved), I sat at a desk with no view other than my laptop and coffee, and solely focused on the chapter I was working on.

I needed to practice this ability to be present with my thoughts and how I would express them on the page, and to block out the lure of checking email or texts, or thoughts about what I was going to make for dinner that night.

Cal Newport writes about the concept of 'shallow work' in his book *Deep Work: Rules for Focused Success in a Distracted World* defining it as "noncognitively demanding, logistical-style tasks, often performed while distracted. These efforts tend to not create much new value in the world and are easy to replicate." Deep work, by contrast, is defined as "Professional activities performed in a state of distraction-free concentration that push your cognitive capabilities to their limit. These efforts create new value, improve your skill and are hard to replicate".[3]

Here's where I think deep work matters in seniors' care. When a situation goes sideways and you do a look back, what often turns up as a lesson learned is that taking the time to assess, discuss, debate and create a solidly thought-through action plan would have prevented the situation.That postmortem may reveal that deep work, allowing yourself the time and space needed to really think before rushing to a decision or action could have altered the outcome and eliminated your regret. This doesn't mean you're going to be right 100% of time if you do the deep work. You will, however, be able to get below the shallow surface of reacting so that you can move onto the next task.

Along with the external stimulation and activity, you've also got what's going on between your ears. Author Ben Hardy writes that, "In 2005, the National Science Foundation published an article showing that the average person has between 12,000 and 60,000 thoughts per day. Of those, 80% are negative and 95% are exactly the same repetitive thoughts as the day before."[4] Not only is our attention competing with external distractions, but our own never-ending internal dialogue is demanding air time too.

I think of being present as a self-soothing, calming elixir that pushes aside all of the distractions and plants us firmly in what's happening in this current moment.

As you read these words, feel how this book sits in your hands, notice where you're sitting and then remark on your breathing - it is shallow or is it deep? Notice if there's tension in your face, and if so, relax your facial muscles. That was about ten seconds of practicing presence.

The Gifts of Presence

THERE ARE some personal benefits from practicing presence: strengthening your brain's ability to focus and pay attention, increasing your happiness while decreasing stress and anxiety, and differentiating yourself and building stronger connections with others.

Just notice the pace and transactional nature that our world continues to encourage, with the need for speed and efficiency. Our phones can shop for us, our laptops bring us the newspaper, and other tech conveniences eliminate the interactions that were once common daily occurrences.

We are sucking the relational out of relationships and becoming purveyors of transactionships.

In a busy, distracted and transactional world that's zigging, you can zag by being present. This is a way to really differentiate yourself and your home with your new families, who have likely cycled through the busyness and distraction of the health care system and have possibly felt handled, processed and dealt with– and give them a much better, richer and heartfelt experience.

Let's look at how being present is also a way to build trust.

Would you agree that when a resident's family trusts you, that it creates a more positive relationship with them?

Amy Cuddy, a social psychologist and Harvard Business School professor, perhaps best known for her TED talk[5] and the power pose – wrote in her book *Presence*[6] that people ask two key questions:

"Can I trust this person?" and "Can I respect this person?" Cuddy writes, "from an evolutionary perspective, it is more crucial to our survival to know whether a person deserves our trust."[7]

We might prefer to believe that competence is the key predictor of how people react to us – but actually warmth, (or trustworthiness) is the most important factor in how people evaluate each other. Competence is evaluated only after trust is established.

Do you remember how I shared earlier that we spent eighteen months chasing down a diagnosis for Ty's illness? We saw twenty-seven doctors, who were mostly specialists, during that time, including a few neurologists and neurosurgeons. We met with one of the best neurosurgeons in Canada. He introduced himself saying, "I'm one of the best head cutters there is." Nice. I had no doubt he was extremely competent (and had the ego to match). I respected his ability to do his job well. But I didn't trust him. Perhaps it was because the surgeon was blunt, but I think I didn't trust him because he wasn't picking up on the terror we were feeling. Without the trust, his competence didn't matter.

Think of it this way. When you are being present with someone, you are likely to be more focused on them, engaged in the conversation, which signals that you are interested in them. By showing this interest in them, you are creating a connection. When you are creating a connection, you are in essence building trust with them. Being present is a way you earn trust with people.

Let's look at other ways you can build trust through your presence.

A simple way is to make a promise, then deliver on that promise.

When you promise to provide the family with information they have asked for, let them know when they can expect it —when you will get back to them.

When you meet that commitment, you are building trust. You

are also showing them that they are important to you, and that you are credible and reliable. Their trust will follow.

Conversely, if you make a promise or commit to something and don't follow through, it could be for a number of reasons. Perhaps you made the promised to appease them, to end the conversation. Or you intended to follow through, but because of distraction and the rushing of doing other things, you simply forgot. By forgetting, which can happen when you fail to be present, your mind went to other more appealing or urgent things.

Haven't you had the experience of being surprised when someone actually followed through on something they would do?

When we don't follow through, we are damaging our reputation and building distrust. And interestingly enough, distrust carries more weight in the brain because of what's called the negativity bias —we are more sensitive to negative experiences and hold on to their memory longer than pleasant memories. I know you have examples of this in your own lives.

While visiting my mom in assisted living one day I took the opportunity to clean up her closet. I had recently bought her a few new pairs of pants and I couldn't find any of them. The only pair of pants she had were the ones she was wearing. I spoke with a staff member at the nurse's station who offered to check with the afternoon shift that was coming in shortly. She asked for my phone number and told me she would call me that night to give me an update. Guess what? No call. Even if she had called to say they couldn't find them or had no further update, I would have been impressed that she did what she said she would do.

These are little things but make a big difference. And the reason they are a big deal is because the follow through would have shown me that I was being listened to, my concerns were important to that staff member, and quite frankly, it would have built up the credibility and trust. And think about how quickly broken promises or lack of follow through can add up, and next thing you know, the family seems to be 'over-reacting' to something you consider small, but it's the build up, the last straw, that triggers a potential disproportionate response.

I think that being attentive is a powerful way to differentiate yourself from others, especially in the context of our changing society. Paying attention with new families will ultimately lead to strong connections with them and will improve the atmosphere of the home for everyone.

When you are fully present you are creating an environment of trust, respect and partnership.

You can help the family feel like they are the most important people to you in that moment, and not just a task or a transaction to be processed, by being intentional about the way you engage with them. Your presence is contributing to how they are feeling about this experience with you, your home, and this new and important relationship.

Have you ever experienced this in admissions meetings, or other meetings with family? Maybe they don't start on time, the team enters and leaves while the discussion is happening. Maybe even side bar conversations happen. Papers are flipped, lots of data is being exchanged, mobile devices are being checked when they ping, and the comings and goings outside the room pull away the gaze of those around the table. And all of this frenetic energy is likely feeding into the anxiety the family already feels.

Perhaps you have overheard, or yourself been the person who complains how a new family admission is going to eat up three hours of the work day. And if you've overheard that, who else in the home can hear that? I understand the frustration, because new family admissions are a lot of work! Whether you embrace or resist this new admission, it's going to happen. And it needs to happen as a big part of running and working in seniors' care. So why not shift your perspective from something that 'has to get done' to something 'you get to do'? Reframed, the move in day meeting is actually a privilege to be able to help a family and resident ease into this new way of life. When you think about it this way – as something you 'get to do', have the privilege to be a part of, you are choosing how you want to approach this and influence those around you. Start with being present and acknowledge with sensitivity and reverence this significant transition for the family.

Judith E. Glaser, in her book *Conversational Intelligence* writes: "When someone shows concern for us, our brain chemistry makes a shift. We become calmer, we regain our composure, and we can begin once again to think in a constructive way."[8]

When you are able to show concern by noticing and responding to the emotions that are present - to feel and share empathy and compassion – you are building a state of trust and rapport – a connection.

When I left Ty at the nursing home that day, driving home alone I was struck by the significance of this change to our lives. I felt overwhelmed with anxiety and sadness, wading into the mire of guilt that families likely feel when this kind of decision needs to be made. I felt very disconnected and disoriented with this change.

I wondered if the staff actually cared about us. We were just trying to cope with what was happening to us as a family. I wondered if they'd noticed the angst that I felt in the meeting. I doubted it, because they were so focused on the tasks at hand. If they had been able to notice and show concern it could have created an opportunity for the trust and connection to start.

I think that moment of recognition and empathy could have led to an even more powerful conversation. Looking back now, there was something I would have really appreciated receiving that evening, or even the next day: a phone call.

I would have really liked it if someone called me that night to say something like, "Today must have been a tough day for you - I can't imagine how hard that was for you". Or to ask, "How are YOU doing? How are the kids doing? How can we support you?"

In my consulting work, families consistently tell me how devastated they felt when they walked out those front doors, leaving their loved one in their new home. Most barely make it to their car without breaking down in tears. A connection can be made during a really tough time. Family members have just had to follow through on a gut-wrenching decision to have their loved one move into a building with lots of other residents who need care, who can no longer live at home or be kept in hospital. The family member has possibly returned home alone. And if their loved one was a spouse or parent who lived with them, they're returning to the emptiness this move has created.

Some families have shared that for those first few days, they keep looking at the time, and wonder what their loved one is doing. They're wondering if they're in the dining room having a meal, if they're engaged with activities, if the staff are helping them and getting to know their routines and preferences. They're wondering if their loved one is safe, feeling scared, adapting to their new surroundings and all of the strangers that are now their house mates. Some families say they don't want to call the home and be a nuisance. They know the staff are busy and don't want the relationship to start off on the wrong foot. But they are worried, feeling guilty and wishing it hadn't come to this. Here they are not knowing what's happening and trying to make sense of the blur of the last few days, while they are also trying to adjust to their new normal, new routines and new identity as a resident's family member.

It's also important to note that the level of angst, worry and fear can also be influenced by where the resident is moving from. For example, it can be a drastic change for a loved one to be moving out of their familial home right into long-term care, compared to someone who has lived in retirement, or assisted living. Moving from one communal living space to another may not be as emotionally challenging initially. It could also be a welcome move if, for example, their loved one was coming from a hospital room, or worse, on a gurney in a hospital hallway.

I know how busy your long-term care homes are, but I also believe when you invest time up front to be really present and build a strong connection with your families, this effort will save you time and frustration in the long run.

Here's one way to look at it. As I shared earlier, when you signal interest in the other person, it fosters a connection that leads to trust, the foundation for any relationship. When family members are connected and feel they have a relationship with you they are going to feel much more settled and a bit more comfortable about their situation which will make them more likely to communicate with you calmly and patiently and to give you the benefit of the doubt when issues arise. There is a much less likelihood of a concern becoming a complaint that spirals into a time-consuming process of investigation and a state of reaction and defensiveness when families feel some level of connection to you.

While there is a business reason to be present, there's also an altruistic aspect that brings us back to the oxytocin that I mentioned in the Eyes chapter. When we are kind and feel compassion for people, we get a boost of the feel-good hormone. We can't help but feel good ourselves. It's like how the saying goes 'you get what you give'. Or 'the quickest way to feel good is to do good'.

Seniors' care homes that I have consulted in, that have embraced the practice of calling family members the evening of admission day have shared inspiring stories of connection and heart felt emotion. Kate, who is an Administrator told me how much it affected her, being able to make such a positive impact with one of their new families. That day, the staff welcomed their new resident, a gentleman in his 80s who was quite frail. His son and daughter-in-law brought him and were taken through the admissions process. Kate could sense the angst the couple were having and made note to check in on them that night. First, she checked in with the home to see how the resident was doing. Then she called the family's home. They had just finished their dinner when she reached them, and the daughter-in-law shared that they were just talking about how tough the day was, and hoping their father was settling in. Kate was able to assure her with a little update on her father-in-law, and then asked how she and her husband were doing.

The daughter-in-law paused with some disbelief that this conversation was even happening. She worked in acute care and knew all too well the transactional aspect of health care. She was overwhelmed with the kindness that was being extended to her on this brief ten-minute call. As much as this was a sad evening for them, and a lot to process, what blew her away was that this staff person took the time to care, to reach out, to not only update them, but to offer her compassion and care by checking in with them as well. The Administrator then shared how every time this family member came to the home, she told every staff she talked to how incredible it was that their Administrator cared enough to call.

A simple gesture can go a long way.

EXPECTATIONS

CREATING WIN/WIN CONVERSATIONS

"Disappointment is the natural result of badly managed expectations."

— CHIP CONLEY

L et's talk about expectations, and how they play into strengthening family relationships. It's so important to be clear with families about what they can expect from you, as well as what you can expect from them.

Check out this formula:

Disappointment = Expectations – Reality
(Chip Conley, *Emotional Equations*)[1]

Have you ever had a family that was surprised when they realized their loved one wasn't getting 24/7, one-on-one care? Or had a family member come to you frustrated that their parent didn't get their bath right at 7:00 pm on the scheduled day? When a family's expectations are different than what is actually occurring, it's a set up for disappointment. And as you well know, their disappointment leads to encounters and sometimes conflicts in your daily work. Focusing on and working toward aligning their expectations as closely as possible to what happens in the reality of the home's operation will help to avoid their disappointment. This is where you come in.

Perhaps you've heard the expression 'don't tell me what I want to hear, tell me the truth.' Sometimes we want to be of service, be so helpful and customer-focused as possible that we fall into the 'people pleaser' mindset. Sound familiar? What happens then is that we find ourselves making commitments or promises that simply can't be fulfilled. In trying to create some ease and comfort to our families, and because the intentions aren't set mindfully, you can bring to life one of my mother's favourite expressions: "The road to hell is paved with good intentions."

My mom moved into retirement - independent living a few years after my dad died, and we expected that she would live there for many years. At about the two and half year mark, her health started deteriorating and it became clear she needed more support. I believe the home staff had the best of intentions to expand their care to the scope we now needed, but we experienced disappointment after disappointment when the gaps became clear and she ended up in hospital due to falling and medication-related issues.

The trust had eroded, our confidence in their abilities evaporated, and we gave our thirty days notice and moved our mom again.

Here's another concept to consider:

"Behind every complaint is an idea, belief or value that person is committed to."[2] (Lisa Laskow Lahey and Robert Kegan)

In the illustration above, I was committed to my mom's safety and comfort and I was looking for the commitment that this organization gave us when my mom selected them as her new home. And if that commitment needed to change based on the changing circumstance, then my belief was that they would approach and educate us on our options. Each side needs to understand the other's expectations.

In Canada, where we have a government-funded health care system, there is an entitlement mentality when it comes to receiving health care. With long-term care, most families know that the government funds a portion of it but they're certainly more aware of the portion they personally need to cover. In retirement living where it's all private pay, the monetary impact is even greater. That creates an elevated expectation of care and service. This is the unknown portion of their expectations, the undercurrent if you will. If you don't know their expectations, and you're not meeting their 'unknown expectations', that's where dissatisfaction can occur – and that can spiral out of control.

The traditional admissions process can tend to be directive in tone with a lot of telling and advising the families about who's who, scripted questions about the resident, and requisite paperwork. This is also an opportunity to understand what perceptions and expectations the family is walking in those front doors with. You can learn a lot just from the questions they are asking, and to really clarify expectations it can be as simple as becoming curious and just asking questions such as:

- Tell us a bit about what your expectations are?
- What are you most worried about with this move?
- What one thing keeps you up at night when you think of your (loved one) living here?
- What's most important to you?
- What do you find yourself hoping for?
- What would you appreciate the most from us?

When you have the family's expectations on the table, you're now better equipped to educate and inform them about what's reasonable and which expectation can be met, and what ones are out of scope for you and your team.

Families share with me that they don't know if their expectations are realistic or not. They come in with hopes based on what friends or family have shared with them and knowing what they've seen about the long-term care business from the news. They would appreciate having someone take the time to really explain how it's going to work. Most families have no experience with long-term care. They are learning as they go. By knowing this you can be proactive with helping them rewrite whatever narrative they come in with through proper education and information sharing.

Get clear on what their expectations are – then you are in a better position to clarify and adjust, and get their expectations and your reality aligned.

Then you're building that pathway to trust. Trust is earned through consistency and follow through, doing what you say you will do, and accepting responsibility and explanation when something falls through the cracks.

Maintaining trust takes ongoing care and focus.

When my mom lived in assisted living, she had a lovely studio suite with a patio door and window that had blinds that could be pulled up and down to control how much light was getting in. I noticed that the blind on the door was breaking regularly - the cord would snap, and the blind would fall, covering the entire door. I had many conversations with various staff members about fixing the blind. What was important to me was that my mom could enjoy the natural sunlight during the day, and she couldn't when the door was covered with the broken blind. It was also important to me that my concerns were being heard. I was starting to feel disappointed and frustrated that what I perceived to be a simple task wasn't being handled.

The last conversation I had was with one of the PSW's on a Saturday morning when I was visiting my mom. I walked into her room and of course the first thing I noticed was the still broken blind. These are the 'stupid little things' that can make family members a bit crazed. I walked over to the nurse's station and one of the PSW's was sitting there - I shared with her that I was feeling a bit frustrated that the blind was still broken. She stood up and said, "Okay, let's go see what's going on." We walked back to my mom's room, she said "Hi" to my mom and told her, "We're gonna get this blind taken care of." The staff member saw the broken cord and said, "I'm going to take this so they can't McGyver it again. They'll have to replace the whole blind and that should do the trick."

I was so impressed with her approach and natural sense of customer service. The following week, there was a new blind up and I was happy not only because it was finally fixed, but that someone cared enough to see this situation through to resolution.

It's usually a simple fix to address family concerns, if you just take the time to:

1. understand what the issue is,
2. communicate with the family what the options are, and,
3. follow through and deliver.

A common theme I hear from families about what creates frustration, and develops into disappointment, is not having information about their loved one shared with them. They feel like they have to ask the questions first, and that's the only way they find out about what's going on with their person and their care.

On a recent visit, Teresa was helping her husband with toileting and discovered that he was wearing a brief. Up to this point, he was wearing regular underwear. As she recounted her story, she was visibly upset about discovering her husband wearing an incontinent product and no one "bothered" to tell her that's what they decided to do.

She told me she "came unglued," speaking out to the PSW, who was desperately trying to calm her down. She felt completely disrespected, and that she should have been consulted about what she saw as a "big deal" decision.

But here's what else happened. She wondered, "what else are

they not telling me?" Not only was she frustrated and disappointed because she felt strongly, and had the expectation that something like this warranted a discussion and joint decision, but now she was questioning whether they were not sharing other important updates.

The trust had been broken, all because of an unmet expectation.

As mentioned earlier, it's a two-way street.

An open, collaborative dialogue about what the expectations are on both sides, can help you create a healthy and effective resolution.

It's appropriate and also necessary that the family is clear on what you expect of them. For example, if they have a concern, how do you want them to share that, and with which team member? If a concern doesn't get resolved to their satisfaction, how do you want them to communicate that? How do you expect them to interact with your front-line staff? What's not okay? (ie. yelling or swearing at staff) I've had staff tell me that they end up tolerating inappropriate behaviour because they didn't want to have things escalate and end up with a formal complaint to the regulatory bodies.

Do you sometimes wonder how you got to the point where toxic behaviour is tolerated? How did that behaviour start in the first place? What were the triggers, and how can you prevent those triggers from happening?

Have you thought about what the ideal family relationship looks like? You know those families, the ones that you look forward to seeing and working with. What makes those relationships work? How can you share with new families what seems to work with other families that they could benefit from knowing about?

Remember, you know your business, your home, what works, and what your challenges are. The best time to set the stage for your new family relationships, including expectations, is at the very beginning. You can take a more proactive approach to onboarding your families with design, versus by default, flying by the seat of

81

your pants, cramming this into an already busy day. You can design this experience with thoughtfulness and intention so that you remove as many knowledge and relational gaps as possible. This way you are setting everyone up for a higher likelihood of success and a pleasant experience for all.

EPILOGUE

Making Moments Matter

This book, and my business was birthed based on my experiences working in seniors' care and as a family member, as well as a passion to help our industry continue to be that lifeline of support for residents and families who need this level of care. There are more than enough challenges and complexities within seniors' care, and that will only continue. Yet there are also opportunities that can be seized every single day to create a memorable moment, with a bit of intention, focus and desire – moments that matter

I want to share what the 'little' moments were for my kids and I– those moments that we still laugh, cry and think fondly about when we get together and raise a toast to their dad, and also when I keynote and conduct workshops, because I believe making moments that matter doesn't have to be rocket science. It doesn't have to take a whole heap of time to do. It's what this book is all about – being mindful and aware. To be empathetic. To care.

- When my daughter Taylor and I would come in together to visit with Ty, more often than not, the female PSW's and registered staff would inevitably tell us 'you two look like sisters'! I could hear that all day long – it never gets old.
- When the staff would help Ty get dressed up for their Hallowe'en celebrations, and take pictures to share with us. I am so grateful that I have those pictures today.
- How Chris would join Ty in the library, where he'd be playing video games (at full volume) and after his shift, on his own time, would play a few games with Chris.
- How Sherry, one of the housekeeping staff, would pull me aside, trying her hardest to tell me a story without breaking out in laughter, about some outlandish thing Ty did – yet again – to keep the management on their toes.
- When one of the staff would see me leaving, head hanging and tears in my eyes – and just come up and give me a hug. No words were needed but I sure felt their empathy.
- When Glen would notice Logan struggling with a tough visit – knowing how hard it was for him to see his dad slowly dying – and he would ask Logan if he'd like to chat 'man to man' for a few minutes.
- When Chris brought Ty an iPod to create a music playlist for him, and he recorded their time together selecting Ty's favourite music. The friendship and pure joy on Ty's face as he played his air guitar while listening to The Eagles is priceless.

WHAT ALL OF these memorable moments have in common is empathy. People noticed and made a choice to reach out, empathize, connect and care. It's really that simple. Those moments that matter still comfort me, and played an immense role in my desire to seek more of them for families like mine.

I created the **RECIPE** framework as a way to help me tell the story of my personal experience as a resident's wife and to equip and empower seniors' care teams to impact and influence the family relationship in a positive and meaningful way.

The RECIPE is bigger than that though. It's really a way to be more relational with anyone – to shift out of that transactional, get-things-done-and-move-on-to-the-next-thing mindset and bring more of who you are as a human being into every encounter. It's about bringing all that potential to connect meaningfully with others, to light. All of these concepts can be applied to any relationship you have – with friends, family, co-workers, and even your coffee shop barista or lunch server. It's a touchstone that can be like a breath of fresh air, a pause of sorts to step back and be more present, aware, and intentional. To be more interested in other people and how they're feeling than perhaps the transaction you're trying to 'get through'.

I'm always thrilled to hear from my clients when they share how the RECIPE framework has helped them build better family relationships and decrease the tension or conflict that they previously felt they just had to endure or manage. I'm so pleased to hear the realization that it's not an accepted part of the seniors' care business that you have to put up with dealing with 'difficult families'. The RECIPE is about a mindset shift, that when you begin the relationship with intention and purpose, preparing your team and the resident's family for a productive and healthy relationship for the time their loved one is living in your home, it the catalyst for a culture transformation in your home.

My consulting work has expanded to *The Family Matters*™ *Program*. It is built on the premise that how you start a relationship will directly influence and impact the quality, trust and respect within that relationship.

New resident admissions are a key event, for both the staff working in the home as well as the family and resident that are impacted. The process alone, from a new resident being selected right through to the six-week care conference, can be anywhere from seventy-five to one hundred process steps. It can be easy to get caught up in the transactional nature and see it as just that – a new admission that needs to get processed.

Along with embracing the **RECIPE** framework as ways of being, we also approach the admissions process as an experience along a continuum of time – from that first call to the family to say there is an available bed, to three months after movie in. There's the practical part of re-designing some of the steps in the process and what I think is even more exciting, is redesigning based on a simple yet powerful lens: how it feels.

When we understand how a certain step in the journey feels, where the moments that matter happen for both the resident and family, as well as the staff, we can then approach this redesign with compassion and empathy. We can look for those opportunities to create positive memories during a potentially sad and stressful time. After all, we remember how people make us feel, not how many boxes got checked off the list. And when there's a mutual understanding that this is a **BIG DEAL** for the families, and the staff are privileged and empowered to be a 'force for good' in this significant time for this family, then the relational approach makes all the difference.

In homes that may be admitting anywhere from twenty to one hundred residents a year, empathy and attentiveness to how people are feeling becomes a powerful lever in culture change. I've seen this happen in homes where we bring the awareness of just how powerful this approach is, and we invite both resident's families and staff to be part of the change we are creating in the ***The Family Matters™ Program***.

After all, we collectively want the same outcome. The families, residents and the staff want the best possible quality of life and care for the resident. And each participant has knowledge, wisdom and desire that will contribute to this, as long as everyone plays nicely in the sandbox together.

How you set up the relationship from the very beginning will determine how the sandbox playing goes.

My wish is that all of us practice the **RECIPE** ingredients, a little bit every day, those principles that inform our small contribution to better experiences and relationships. I hope that we can all be more mindful about the privilege and power to impact and influence other people in a positive and meaningful way, just by how we choose to show up and interact with them, how we choose to be with them.

A MESSAGE FROM TAYLOR

My dad "got sick" when I was sixteen. I put quotations around those two words because Erdheim-Chester isn't an illness you can see right away. It presented itself as a stumble here, a slight slurring of speech there. It wasn't as aggressive as some cancers, and it didn't run rampant through our home like the flu. It was slow and dormant, and for the first little while, my dad was still acting like my dad.

Until he wasn't.

It felt like I blinked, and suddenly he went from walking on his own, to needing a walker. Too often I would come home to find him laying at the bottom of the stairs, because he had fallen there and couldn't get himself back up. Dozens of PSW's, like a revolving door, came through my home to help dad with every day activities he once managed on his own. I would leave my bedroom in the morning trying to get ready for school, and bump into somebody I didn't know. I'll be honest, I was angry. I felt helpless, and it seemed unfair. While other teenage girls were having their dad help them with their car, or intimidating boys that came to their front door to pick them up for a date, mine was having a PSW help him put his socks on. The strong, football-playing, quick-witted man I'd always looked up to was deteriorating before my eyes, and I just didn't know how to handle it. I started spending more time away from home, grasping onto my then boyfriend's family, because they were the 'normal' I craved. There, I didn't have to face my family's life spiraling out of control. Ignorance is bliss, isn't it?

I remember a turning point before my dad was placed into long-term care. I was getting a ride home with a friend, when we turned the corner onto my street. I saw ambulance lights and thought "No way, that's at my house". As we inched closer, I watched paramedics bringing my dad outside on a stretcher. I jumped out of the car as it slowly rolled towards my house and sprinted to my incoherent dad, an oxygen mask on his face. Panicked, I asked the paramedics what was going on, and they didn't have an answer for me. They didn't know what was wrong. Apparently, he had fallen again, but the severity of the fall was unknown. It was blatantly obvious at this point that my dad was no longer able to live in our two-storey side split anymore without risking his safety, and he was placed on the list to live in a nursing home.

As my mom has said—nobody ever dreams of living in a long-term care facility. However, the home where my dad spent the final four years of life was a silver lining in a series of unfortunate events, to say the least. The staff treated my dad like family, often playing Nintendo Wii in the common room with him, or watching his favorite movies. He was given an iPod, where he could close his eyes and recall earlier days in his life while listening to The Eagles. His regular PSW's shared laughs with him, having inside jokes and embracing him playfully. To them, he was more than a resident, and it showed. The staff's passion for their job was especially evident when my family and I visited. I was greeted by name with a big smile almost every time. On more difficult days when I left his room in tears, I was often asked the simple question "are you okay?" or "do you need a hug?" by a member of the staff. The impact of such a 'small' gesture was massive. It didn't feel like I was visiting my dad at some sort of clinical, transactional institution…it felt like a second family. And all of us strived for one common goal—for my dad to have great care and amazing quality of life.

As each year passed, my dad became worse. Eventually, he was completely wheelchair bound and unable to speak much. He was being fed pureed food, because he could no longer eat solid food without choking. I remember sitting in the dining hall with him, assisting as he ate his lunch. Halfway through me giving him a spoonful of something mushy, I broke down. Before I could suck them back into my eyes, tears were spilling down my cheeks, and I placed my face in my hands. I didn't want to show my dad I was upset, so I desperately tried pulling it together before he, or anyone else noticed. After all, Ty hated seeing his little girl cry…because to him, that's what I still was. His little girl. This was something he had done for me at one point in my life…feed me. Now, there I was, doing the same for him. It seemed life had come full circle, and I wasn't ready for that yet. In that moment, I felt a hand gently squeeze my shoulder. I turned around to see one of my dad's favorite PSW's, who gently told me if I needed a break, she'd be happy to take over for me. It was *that* simple gesture of compassion that distinguished my experience with the staff at my dad's long-term care home…they noticed the little things. Somewhere between doing their job and being human, they created a connection with people who needed it. To me, that's pretty extraordinary.

My dad passed away on Monday April 6, 2015. The morning we received that phone call, that he had slipped into unconsciousness through the night, we were all taken aback. We all knew this day would come, and for years, we *thought* we were mentally prepared. However, when that day arrived, prepared wasn't the emotion we felt. My whole family and I sat in a private room with my dad while he remained 'comfortable'. The staff brought a speaker in so we could play The Beatles for him. They brought in coffee and sandwiches, reminding us "You need to eat". They held our hands, offered prayers, and consistently checked in without being over-bearing. After my dad had taken his final breath, everybody cleared the room and I was left alone with him. I held his hand and placed my head on his chest. After I said my last goodbye, I walked into the hall where a member of the maintenance staff (and I will stress the importance of this, because he had *zero* obligation to our family) embraced me tightly, and cried with me. We had almost all my dad's closest staff attend his funeral, one of them even took the time to speak. The love, empathy and compassion the staff showed my dad, me and my family while he lived in the home was what made an awful and dark situation better. It was the difference between transactional and relational.

Thank you, to all the staff at my dad's home. You know who you are.

The Bakti Family. Photo By Brooks Reynolds

NOTES

INTRODUCTION

1. Ontario Long-Term Care Association. "This is Long-Term Care 2018 report. https://www.oltca.com/OLTCA/Documents/ Reports/ThisIsLongTermCare2018.

2. THE ROAD TO THE RECIPE

1. Steve Jobs, Stanford Commencement Address. June 12, 2005. https://news. stanford.edu/news/2005/june15/jobs-061505.

3. FIRST IMPRESSIONS

1. Maya Angelou

4. RESET

1. Jill Bolte Taylor, *My Stroke of Insight: A brain scientist's personal journey*. New York: Penguin Books, p.126.
2. Eric L. Garland, Barbara Frederickson, Ann M. Kring, David P. Johnson, and Piper S. Meyer. "Upward spirals of positive emotions counter downward spirals of negativity: Insights from the broaden-and-build theory and affective neuroscience on the treatment of emotion dysfunctions and deficits in psychopathology." *Clinical Psychology Review*, 2010. Vol. 30:7 p. 845-64.
3. Linda Stone. "Constant Partial Attention". https://lindastone.net/qa/ continuous-partial-attention/
4. Ethan Kross, Emma Bruehlman-Senecal, Jiyoung Park , Aleah Burson , Adrienne Dougherty, Holly Shablack , Ryan Bremner, Jason Moser , Ozlem Ayduk. "Self-talk as a Regulatory Mechanism: How you do it matters".
    Journal of Personality and Social Psychology, 2014 Feb;106(2). p. 304-24
    https://www.academia.edu/32400116/Self-talk_as_a_regulatory_mechanism_How_you_do_it_matters

5. EYES

1. Mark Bowden. "Step Reading and Start Leading," https://www.theartof.com/ articles/stop-reading-and-start-leading-mark-bowden/. October 15, 2015

2. Sherry Turkle. "Stop Googling. Let's Talk." *New York Times*. September 27, 2015. https://www.nytimes.com/2015/09/27/opinion/sunday/stop-googling-lets-talk/. September 27, 2015.

3. Douglas Stone and Sheila Heen. *Thanks for the Feedback The Science and Art of Receiving Feedback Well.* New York: Penguin Books, 2015.

6. CURIOSITY

1. Gary E. Swan and Dorit Carmelli. "Curiosity and Mortality in Aging Adults: A 5-year follow-up of the Western Collaborative Group Study. *Psychology and Aging, 1996* 11(3) p. 449-53.

2. Jason Piccone. "Curiosity and Exploration". http://www.csun.edu/~vcpsy00h/students/curious/. Spring 1999.

3. Todd B. Kashdan and Michael Steger. "Curiosity and pathways to well-being and meaning in life: Traits, states, and everyday behaviour. *Motivation and Emotion.*2007 31(3):159-173.

4. Online dictionary. https://www.dictionary.com/browse/judgment

5. Karen Reivich, and Andrew Shatte. *The Resilience Factor: 7 Keys to Finding Your Inner Strength and Overcoming Life's Hurdles.* New York: Broadway Books, 2002

7. INTENTION

1. Jane Goodall. https://www.goodreads.com/quotes/159740-what-you-do-makes-a-difference-and-you-have-to/.

2. Matthew A. Killingworth and Daniel T. Gilbert. "Wandering Mind Not A Happy Mind". *Harvard Gazette.* November 2010.

8. PRESENT

1. MINDmgt.com, "Focus".

2. Francisco Cirillo. *Pomodoro Technique.* FC Garage GmbH, 2013.

3. Cal Newport. *Deep Work.* New York: Grand Central Publishing Hachette Book Group

4. Benjamin Hardy. *"To Have What You Want, You Must Give-Up What's Holding You Back." Medium.* June 9, 2018.

5. Amy Cuddy. TedX talk. "Your body language may shape who you are." 2012. https://www.ted.com/talks/amy_cuddy_your_body_language_shapes_who_you_are?language=en/

6. Amy Cuddy. *Presence Bringing your boldest self to your biggest challenges.* New York: Hachette Book Group, 2015.

7. Amy Cuddy. *Presence.*

8. Judith E. Glaser. *Conversational Intelligence: How great leaders build trust and get extraordinary results.* New York: Bibliomotion. Inc., 2014. p 35.

9. EXPECTATIONS

1. Chip Conley. *Emotional Equations; Simple Truths for Creating Happiness + Success.* New York: Free Press, 2012. p. 47.
2. Lisa Laskow Lahey and Robert Kegan. How the Way We Talk Can Change the Way We Work: Seven Languages for Transformation. Jossey-Bass, 2002.

ACKNOWLEDGMENTS

While I was in the midst of becoming and being a resident's wife I never imagined I'd be writing a book about the experience and lessons learned. As the entrepreneurial dreamer, Ty always wanted to be successful enough so that I could 'quit my job and write my book'. I've done that now. I know he would be pleased. We never know how our wishes are granted, nor can we predict how our lives will twist and turn, but we do have control over how we respond to what life gives us.

To my kids Taylor and Logan – who endured the unthinkable and are such incredible humans – thank you for sticking together, for understanding that 'adversity builds character', and supporting me through my career shift from corporate to business owner.

To Ty's family – Helen and Ken Burley, and 'Grandma Sopo' – as you navigated through your loss you made space for ours with love and support.

There were so many people at Extendicare that I worked with who supported me during our darkest days, both emotionally and navigationally. I couldn't possibly name you all individually and remember everyone, so I'm acknowledging you collectively. Having my career take a turn into seniors' care was no accident – I just couldn't see it at the time. I am incredibly grateful for the teams I worked with, led and felt supported by, both within corporate office and in the homes and home care locations.

This book wouldn't be in your hands if it weren't for Patti M. Hall, my book coach and editor. The idea of writing a book is much more alluring than the actual practice and persistence needed to get the concepts onto the page. Her encouragement and insistence that I keep going made all the difference.

To my friends, Liz Long, Heidi Cowie, Donna Corbett – who tolerated my passion (or obsession) with this work, and provided their encouragement, insights and feedback – so grateful.

And to my seniors' care clients, staff and families who shared with me their stories, insights, wishes and suggestions, so that I could achieve this book's intention of creating better outcomes and experiences for everyone on both sides of this key relationship could be strengthened.

To Chris Poos, who was Ty's "#1 friend" and supporter at the home – thank you for your compassion and for your friendship. You exemplify what it means to care.

Ty was the eternal optimist, and we were all convinced that he would live forever. I believe he would be happy to know that his spirit lives on, and that he is a part of a movement to transform the experience of families to shift from enduring to perhaps (imagine) embracing.

Learn more about how the RECIPE and other program offerings
can help your Seniors' Care organization
at
www.deborahbakti.com

CPSIA information can be obtained
at www.ICGtesting.com
Printed in the USA
LVHW081958130619
621144LV00010B/12/P

9 781999 162115